Humbled and Exalted

One Woman's Journey to Biblical Womanhood

KIMBERLY M. TAYLOR

www.humbledandexalted.com

CrossBooks™
A Division of LifeWay
1663 Liberty Drive
Bloomington, IN 47403
www.crossbooks.com
Phone: 1-866-879-0502

First published by CrossBooks 6/30/2011

ISBN: 978-1-6150-7867-7 (sc)
ISBN: 978-1-6150-7868-4 (hc)

Library of Congress Control Number: 2011928983

Printed in the United States of America

This book is printed on acid-free paper.

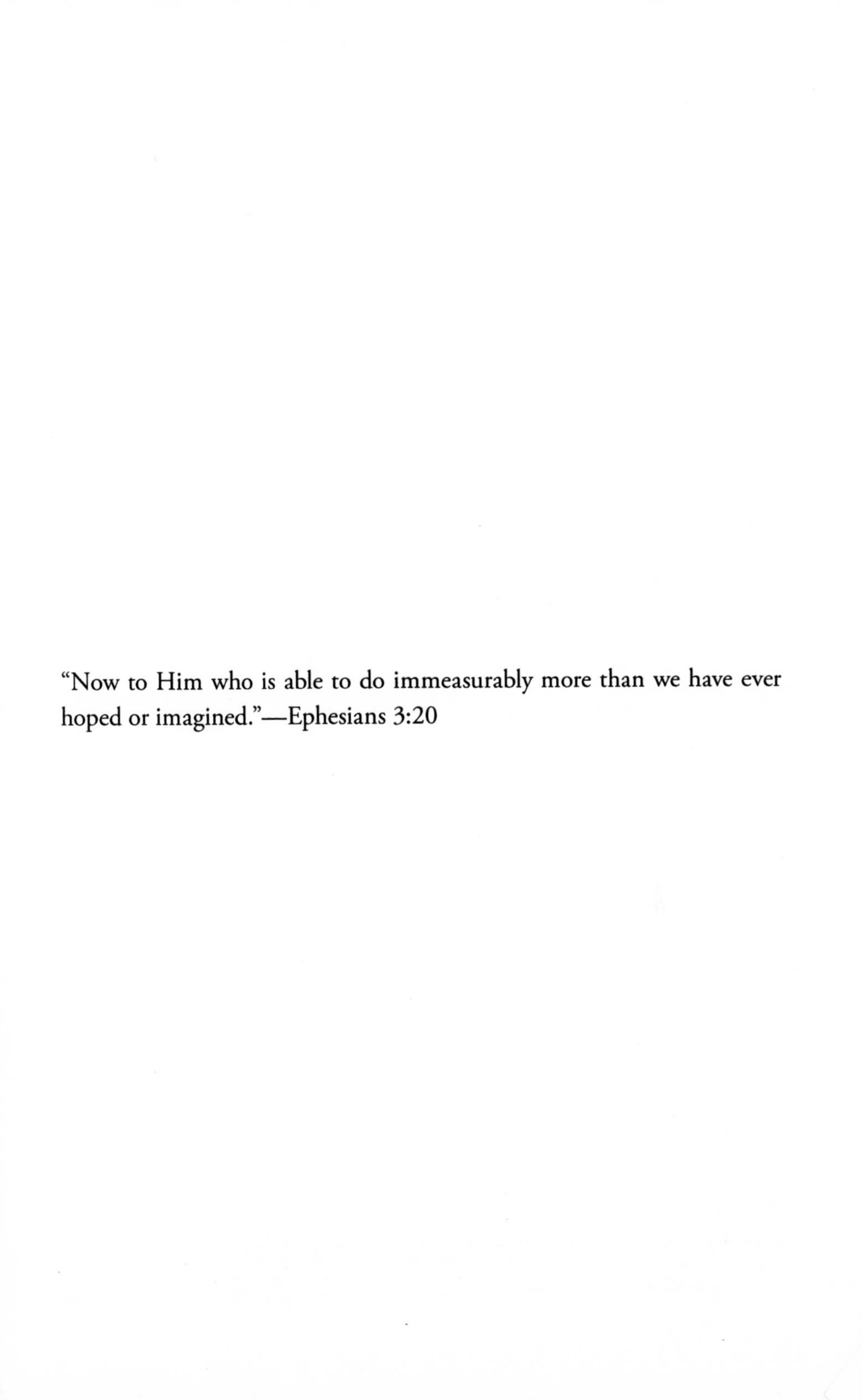

"Now to Him who is able to do immeasurably more than we have ever hoped or imagined."—Ephesians 3:20

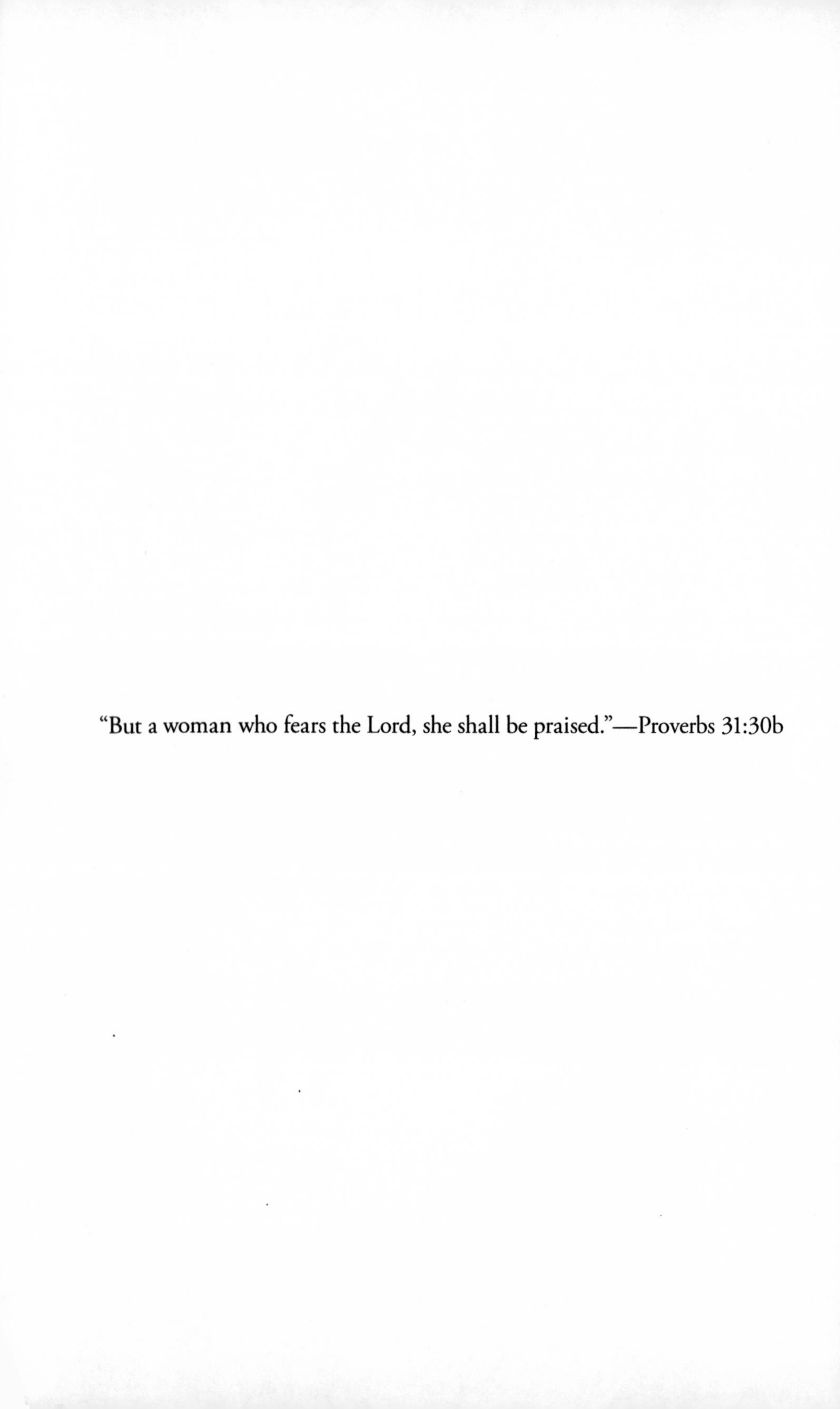

"But a woman who fears the Lord, she shall be praised."—Proverbs 31:30b

Contents

Foreword

"That they may teach younger women to be ..." Such a small book of the Bible, Titus nonetheless has a powerful call to ministry. This excerpt, from Titus 2:4, is a call for older women to teach younger women the ways of the Lord.

When we were first married, my wife, Kim, had a vision to write a book from her journal about God's work in and through her life. A life, like most, with hills and valleys.

As Kim wrote this book, we prayed over its completion and that it would impact the hearts and souls of women for generations to come. This book embodies God's call for older women to teach younger women. I pray that Kim's life story, along with the Holy Spirit's shaping of her, encourages, challenges, and convicts you while reading this book.

Kim's life as told in this book is proof of this passage from 2 Timothy 3:16–17: "All Scripture is given by inspiration of God, and is profitable for doctrine, for reproof, for correction, for instruction in righteousness: that the man of God may be perfect, thoroughly furnished unto all good works."

The Holy Spirit molded my wife into a strong woman of God, and I hope He richly touches your life through this book as well.

May God bless you!

Steven Taylor

Preface

Humbled and Exalted is the story of my journey to biblical womanhood. I wrote the book with the hope of encouraging women to embrace the lifestyle that God has created for us. Biblical womanhood is the first step to an abundant life. My journey started out in an "unequally yoked" marriage and proceeds through my first husband's adultery and our divorce after years of his infidelity, God's restoration of my life, and a miraculous second marriage. When I was in my unequally yoked marriage, I could not find any books to assist me. I just wanted to read that someone else had survived the same situation. I did not want to pursue divorce, and I needed a resource to help me in my current marriage.

I never found those written resources, but the Lord brought mentors into my life who brilliantly explained biblical womanhood to me as it is taught in the Scriptures. I embraced the concepts, and the Lord performed amazing works in my life as I applied biblical truths. As a result, I have now written this book to provide encouragement to other women in any marital situation (married, single, or divorced), or those who just want to learn about biblical womanhood regardless of their marital situation.

Introduction

I was the typical twenty-five-year-old working woman in many ways. My story starts about six months into my first marriage. I thought I was living the "American Dream." I was working full time, attending college to get my degree, and enjoying marriage to my high-school sweetheart. As you read my story, you will find many twists, turns, and surprises along the way that completely changed my life in every way.

I had decided not to attend four years of college right out of high school. I thought it would be better to move away from home and start supporting myself as soon as possible. In many ways, this was the best decision I made. In many other ways, this was the worst decision I made.

Worldly wisdom and experience had also led me to making poor financial choices. At this point in my life, I finally purchased a house after several years of paying rent to make other people rich. I had purchased several brand new cars one after the other, all on credit. I obtained several credit cards and could purchase whatever I wanted and barely gave excessive spending a second thought. I also gave my husband a credit card in my name. While my purchases were for small items, he liked to buy and sell large items such as cars. I had a good job at a prestigious law firm where I could clock as much overtime as I wanted and easily worked sixty to eighty hours every week. Between my car loans and other unsecured credit, I had easily incurred $30,000 in credit card and car loan debt. I was lucky if I could make more than the minimum payment each month. Some of the debt had interest rates between 18 and 21 percent. The answer to this financial crisis always seemed to lie in getting another credit card or unsecured loan to pay off something else.

As my story begins, I was experiencing another typical day. The alarm clock went off to start my morning. I was sleeping alone in my bed. My dog, a beautiful black Akita who would give her life to protect me was sleeping at the foot of the bed. We had a special bond. My husband brought her home to be his dog, but she bonded with me the second she entered the house. We quietly walked through the small one-story house so she could go outside without waking my brother-in-law, who was sleeping in one bedroom, or my husband, who was sleeping on the couch. After letting the dog out, I took a shower, ate breakfast, let the dog back in, and left for work.

I have a vivid memory of waking my husband the night before and asking him to come to bed because he had fallen asleep on the couch. His response was that he would be there after one last cigarette. However, every night we went through this routine, and he never seemed to make it to bed. I wondered whether something was wrong with our relationship.

My husband and I were best friends when dating and living together. Now we were no longer best friends, and it seemed as if I had become the "mom" to his "rebellious child." We hardly spoke to each other, and we never did anything together anymore. My brother-in-law, Jacob, who was eight years younger than us, had moved into the house. Even though my husband promised things would not change, he was now a stranger. We had established the rules for Jacob to move in. My husband had promised—prior to him moving in—that if there was ever a disagreement, he would always take my side. This was the first of many promises to be broken. Now it seemed they spent all their waking hours together away from the house until I went to bed at night.

I slept alone night after night. The routine was always the same. I would get up about 1:00 AM and ask him to come to bed. He would say okay and never make it. I couldn't keep getting up, as I had to get ready for work the next day. He did not have to get up since he was not working. So it was easy for him to ignore my requests to come to bed. Then the excuse changed to the bed not being comfortable due to his car accident.

Eventually I just stopped asking. I spent my day at work with no word from him and returned home to an empty house.

I let the dog out and then went to the gym for up to an hour and a half of my weight lifting routine or go to the cycling or kickboxing classes. My looks were important to me and exercise was a great stress relief. These classes were the only way I could be motivated to do my cardiovascular exercise.

My looks and worldly dress were important to my husband; he valued these much more than my personality or character.

After working out, I returned home and prepared a nice meal. I fixed my plate, turned on the TV, and ate dinner with my dog sitting at my feet. Tired and alone, I went to bed wondering if this is what God had in mind for marriage. How could a married person be so lonely? Around midnight or so, I would hear my husband and brother-in-law coming in from socializing or working on cars with his friends. They ate the dinner I left for them. My husband would then fall asleep on the couch. He did not work, so his time in the evenings was also his excuse for contributing to the household income by buying and selling whatever he could. It usually ended up being cars. Other than the rent paid by my brother-in-law, I never benefited from those earnings. In this household, I was the primary breadwinner. I would tell my friends, "I bring home the bacon, cook it, and clean up the frying pan too."

Once or twice a week, my husband and I had an evening together. This was to primarily meet his physical needs. While we had no friendship, I still felt that my obligation to him was to fulfill my marriage commitments in every way. I felt in my heart there was something wrong with this. Many of our friends seemed to have better marriages. I noticed that their husbands were home for dinner and stayed home in the evenings. Their husbands did not seem to detest being at home. Many times, I missed having a grown man who was committed to loving and cherishing me for the rest of my life. I did not feel loved or cherished.

Fall came around again, and it was time to rake leaves. We had a three quarter acre lot that would accumulate two inches of oak leaves in a week. First I started the lawnmower and mowed the leaves into a mulch pile. Since I now had years of practice at doing yard work alone, I found this would take ten bags of whole leaves and turn it into one bag of mulch. I didn't have a truck, so I had to bag leaves for the trash to pick up. I would rake about fifteen bags of leaves a week, and the trash people could pick up five. Before the lawnmower technique, I easily bagged forty to fifty bags each week, and they sat along the length of the driveway until the garbage truck eventually picked them up. Each fall, my leaf routine would last three to four weekends in a row. The weather was usually pleasant this time of year, and I enjoyed being outside. My husband would not be home as he hated yard work and would always find something else to do.

I worked around the junk cars in the yard, the trucks that were off their frames, or the oil spots. One time someone complained, and the local building inspector came out to write a ticket. It seemed to neighbors that our household took no pride in our living conditions. If only they could see the hidden secrets of the heart. The inner turmoil of this home boiled over to the outside as well.

In addition to the yard work, I did all the housework. I cleaned the house from top to bottom, did laundry and put it away (including my husband's), did the dishes, and did anything else that needed to be done to maintain a clean household. There seemed to be something wrong with this situation, and I did not know how to fix it. The advice from friends was to get a divorce. They would say, "You deserve better than this," or "Why do you put up with him?" I didn't have an answer.

We had several sets of friends who we had socialized with over the years. Many times we drove separately to those places due to our schedules, even though he rarely held a job. One set of friends included my best friend from high school. We had two other sets of individuals who were close friends and traveling buddies. All would tell me I deserved better. Even the individuals who we met through my husband did not think it was a good relationship for me. We had lost friends because they thought the relationship was so bad.

Every day I desired to be in a different situation. I felt trapped. I felt there was no way out. I had made a lifelong promise to love this person, but this person had changed. This person seemed to be someone different than the person I had married. I wanted my best friend back, but that person no longer seemed to exist.

Chapter 1

The Wisdom of the World

My mind raced. How had I gotten here? How did I go from being saved and loving God to being in a terrible marriage to an unbeliever? Where had all this debt come from? A good majority of the debt was not even mine. Was this really God's plan for my life? Was God really sovereign? It would take years for me to find the answers to these questions.

When I was in kindergarten, I attended a Christian school. We went to chapel every Wednesday. One day, during chapel, the preacher was talking about John 3:16, which says, "For God so loves the world that he gave his only begotten Son that whosoever believes in Him should not perish, but have everlasting life." John 3:18 goes on to say, "He who believes in Him is not condemned; but he who does not believe is condemned already." I went forward for salvation that day. I was so excited that I even told my neighborhood friend about it, and she wanted salvation too. I had a pretty innocent upbringing and stayed in Christian school until the eighth grade.

During my junior high school years, my closest friends left Christian school to attend public school, and there were some challenges at my church. My mother had emergency surgery, and no one from the church ever came to visit her. My parents didn't go to church for a while as a result. By the time they started looking for another church, I wasn't interested. During that same time, I remember begging for years to go to the public high school. I was tired of being different and not having any friends close by. So they relented and sent me to public high school. I faced many challenges that first year. Christian school had taught me book knowledge about God, but not heart knowledge. I had memorized full chapters of Scripture. They did not teach me to think through what the world would teach about science and what was wrong with it. They just taught me to memorize. So I started a long journey of working out my faith and made poor decisions in the process.

One of my poor decisions was my dating life. When I was fifteen, I started dating someone who was twenty-two. I thought, *I'll date him until someone better comes along.* What fifteen- or sixteen-year-old boy is going to try to compete for the affection of a girl who is dating a twenty-two-year old? Would he be worth having as a boyfriend if he was willing to not respect that I was someone else's girlfriend? I didn't fully realize all this at the time. I just wanted to have some fun and freedom. I thought very highly of myself.

My strong personality was quite a challenge for my parents. I should have known something was wrong with a guy that old being interested in a teenager, but I always liked older boys anyway. My parents and grandparents did not like him; however, the legal statutes in my state were more supportive of the child's rights than the parent's rights. I had not yet learned the lesson of submission or to take advantage of the insights of those who love you. We continued to date for many years and seemed to break up every spring. Then he would come back, saying how much he missed me. I kept taking him back. This pattern lasted into adulthood for ten years.

While working full-time, I obtained my associate's degree in legal assisting at age nineteen. It was time to find a job in my field. I went on several job interviews and finally accepted a position at a large, international law firm.

The day of my job interview is a compelling memory for me. I arrived at the law firm and sat in the reception area, fascinated by the fast-paced comings and goings of the elevators, couriers, and high-priced suits. This law firm was one of the largest in the country and was located right in the middle of historic Richmond, Virginia. The waiting area was as fancy as could be, with green marble floors and gold trim. The couriers came and went as fast as they could just like a scene from TV, and here I was, dressed in my navy suit, trying to get a job as a legal secretary.

Then I got the call: I was hired! After working at this firm for a couple of years, I had earned the respect of those I worked with. I worked sixty to eighty hours a week and made more money than I ever thought possible with an associate's degree. I had been promised a management position in my department the next time one became available. The department was quickly expanding, so I was given the impression that the opportunity would arrive quickly.

At the age of twenty-three, I returned to school to earn my bachelor's degree. It was a program designed for individuals who also worked full-time. I added to my mountain of debt by getting a student loan. I wouldn't have to make payments for a year after finishing college, so it seemed like a good idea at the time.

About a year into the program, I had to take electives. One of the required credits for the degree was a religion class, so I took a class called Survey of the New Testament. The book was a fact-based history course of the New Testament times of Christ. During this class, the Lord slowly started working on my heart. He would say, "Remember me?" and "I'm still here," "Wouldn't you like to go to church again?" and "I never left you." Again and again I would hear these thoughts in my head, and they would not go away. I still trusted that the Lord would save me and believed all the right things about Him.

However, despite my Christian upbringing, I was never taught how to apply Scripture to my life in a practical way. My teachings had been legalistic: "this is right and this is wrong." I did not know how to love Him or have a personal relationship with Him. It was all "head" knowledge.

My husband-to-be and I had been living together off and on since I was nineteen. After taking the New Testament class, I started feeling that living together was wrong. However, I had no idea how to get out of the situation. With the small voice still nagging me, I started pressuring my boyfriend to do the right thing. We needed to get married or break up. I really did not know what the right thing was at this point. I knew the pastor at my parents' church would not marry us, because my boyfriend would not attend church and because we were living together. The pastor felt that a Christian should not marry a non-Christian, and he would not marry two non-Christians. He would also not marry two individuals living together. At the time, I thought he was wrong in his thoughts. I just wanted to correct my sin and thought that the two options would be to get married or break up.

Our wedding day finally arrived. I had the perfect dress, music, and flowers. It was being held at my parents' church with a substitute pastor. It was the perfect wedding to match my personality. There were a few details that just did not seem right. I had always envisioned the bridesmaids surrounding the bride, but my bridesmaids stood out in the parking lot with their husbands the whole time. I was in the room by myself for what seemed like forever. I finally had another friend show up who kept me company. I confided in her that I was really nervous. I thought I had wedding day jitters.

About ten minutes before I walked down the aisle, I was moved to a different room at the back of the church. This moment stands out as a vivid memory of making the choice between two roads. The room I was standing in was a side room in the foyer of the church. To the left of me was the front door of the church where I could just walk right out. To my right was the door that led to the aisle before the altar and the man who said he loved me. I kept thinking over and over and over that I really just wanted to go left and walk out the door. It was such a huge internal battle. At the time I dismissed it as wedding day jitters. This indecision seemed to go on forever.

Then I heard the trumpets sounding from my CD player. At the beginning of the wedding march, my song started with trumpets announcing the bride. It is the same type of trumpet you hear when royalty enters the room. It was time to walk down the aisle. I was so relieved. The battle in my head would now end, and I could keep my commitment to marry this man.

Little did I know this was just the beginning of a battle that would last many years. I also later recognized that my wedding day jitters were the Holy Spirit screaming at me to not go through with the wedding. Since I was not used to following the lead of the Holy Spirit, I did not have enough knowledge to recognize what was going on inside me.

Pastor Randy Hahn of the Colonial Heights Baptist Church in Colonial Heights, Virginia, explained it brilliantly. He explained that once we are saved, the Holy Spirit is sealed inside us. However, we still have to make the choice whether or not to sin. When we sin, the Spirit, who is holy, is still there and is stuck in a sinful body. If we don't repent and ask the Spirit to lead us after we sin, the Holy Spirit's voice becomes less and less important in our lives. He is stuck inside us but does not control us. What happened to me was that the Holy Spirit was trying to lead me, but I chose not to listen. I grieved the Holy Spirit.

Chapter 2
A New Woman

After getting married, I visited my parents' church a couple of times, but I did not feel like I fit in. I was married, but my husband would not even think about setting foot in a church. All of the Sunday school classes were geared towards married couples where both the husband and the wife loved God. The last thing I wanted was to sit there by myself. The subject matter of a Christian married couple would not be the same subject matter that would be of interest to me. Much of the teaching was also geared towards couples with children. My husband and I planned to never have children so I did not want to focus my time on child rearing information. I was also working sixty to eighty hours a week and going to college full-time. How could I possibly have time to go to church? I had to do homework on Sundays. Every excuse in the book came up. But that small voice kept nagging me.

So I started praying: *Lord, show me if I need to change jobs so I can go to church.* I prayed specifically for a job where I could work forty hours a week and be able to go to church. I prayed for this for six months. I promised God that if I changed to a job where I only had to work forty hours a week, I would start looking for a church where I was comfortable.

By this point, I had graduated college and was receiving insults from my coworkers for having a college degree. I kept hearing that all of my hard work meant nothing and that only on-the-job experience was valuable. They would tell me I should not have wasted so much time and money on a piece of paper. I had put in a lot of sweat and hours to make that degree happen, and I would hear at least weekly that it meant nothing. So my job started getting more and more frustrating. I was counting on the promise from my superiors and manager that I could climb the corporate ladder. But that never materialized. Other people got the promotions I had been promised. In addition, the stress at work was building. The last straw was when I started having chest pains. I was about twenty-five years old and having chest pains. This was not a good situation, and my supervisor sent me home.

That day, I checked online for a job. I had been looking off and on but not seriously. I saw an opening for a staff auditor with a local government agency I had been watching as a potentially good employer. It was local government, which I knew meant forty hours a week, and it was close to home and looked like an interesting career opportunity. It also required a bachelor's degree and CPA license. I had the degree and had recently made the decision to start pursuing my license. The problem was, the opportunity to apply for it closed at 5:00, which just allowed me two hours to submit the application. I did not have my résumé done, and I did not have an application to fill out. I rushed through updating my résumé with my past three years' experience, and I rushed to the local office to fill out the application. It was 4:55 when I turned it in. The Lord answered my prayer. In just six short weeks, I was working at my new job.

All the time I had been thinking about changing jobs and wondering which church to attend, God was at work behind the scenes at my parents' church. The pastor was still single when I had last visited. He met the love of his life during this timeframe, and she had a degree from the seminary that specialized in learning about "biblical womanhood." This phrase was brand new to me.

She started a class just for women, married and single. So I decided to pay a visit. There were just a few of us in the class that day. I met a woman named Katrina who was also married. Her husband went to a different Sunday-school class. Katrina was interested in attending this class. We instantly hit it off and were the best of friends right from the start. We had a great conversation that Sunday, and I felt comfortable in the class as a result. Katrina and I had similar interests including politics, were brand new in our marriages, and our personalities allowed us to become instant friends.

The teacher's name was Ashley. She was several years younger than me, and I wondered whether someone younger could teach me. From a personality and interest comparison, she was also quite different from me. I was more of a tomboy, and she was as girlie girl as they came. However, once she started teaching, she was eloquent in her delivery of the material. She was passionate about biblical womanhood. She was the first person I met who was passionate about this subject, which I knew little about. She described herself as a leader and very strong-willed, and according to the world's definition, that should clash with biblical womanhood. I was glad to see we had those personality traits in common, as I was also strong-willed and independent. I could relate to many of the stories and challenges she told. I could also respect her position on things, such as submission. If anyone else had tried to teach that concept to me, I don't think I would have embraced the idea. She did a brief introduction of women's roles in marriage, the church, and other areas of life. I wasn't sure about everything she was saying, but I related to her being a strong leader and strong-willed. I was curious to see what else she had to say about biblical womanhood.

I started attending church every Sunday. It was not easy going by myself, but I always felt better when I left. I walked in the door each Sunday feeling like I had a fifty-pound bag of potatoes on my back from the stresses of the week. Each Sunday, I left feeling like the bag weighed only ten pounds. It never completely went away, but my two hours at church energized me for the week ahead.

My husband was glad I was so committed to going to church, as it got me out of the house and out of his hair a few hours on the weekend. He could actually spend some time at the place he called home without a nagging wife there trying to engage him and be part of his life.

Katrina and I continued to become better friends. My respect for Ashley the teacher continued to grow. The Sunday-school class grew, and I made more friends. No one ever knew all that I was going through, as I never completely opened up. I was like a sponge, absorbing everything

Ashley taught. All of the ladies seemed to be. None of us had ever really had such great teaching about biblical womanhood. The most awesome thing was that Ashley and Steven (the pastor), who were married, not only taught the Bible, they lived it. Ashley never said anything negative about Steven. She was a living representation of a godly wife. And Steven was the living representation of a godly husband. Their love for God and each other overflowed in their lives. I always wished that God had chosen a similar path for me. I was still going to church by myself and had accepted the idea but always wished I could have my husband in church with me as well.

Through Ashley's teaching, I finally understood the concept of being "unequally yoked." Growing up, I had learned this term to be in relation to race, not religion. I think that is a faux pas of one of my southern pastors of about twenty years ago. But Ashley explained that in the day of Christ, many farmers would use oxen to pull the plow through the ground. If one ox was bigger than the other, the plow would not pull equally. Both the bigger ox and the smaller ox would have huge open sores on their skin from rubbing if they plowed together, because the yoke would not sit correctly on either of them. Since I was now in an unequally yoked marriage, I could relate to what she was teaching. I did feel like I had huge open sores all over me on a daily basis from trying to build a life with someone who didn't seem to even like me anymore.

Understanding this concept was a turning point in my life. I really did not want to be married to an unbeliever. I was tired of being so miserable in my marriage. I wanted a husband who would come to church with me. However, I also wanted to do what God wanted me to do. So for the first time, I turned to the Bible to find out what it said about marriage and divorce.

First I found I Corinthians 7:13–14: "And a woman who has a husband, who does not believe, if he is willing to live with her, let her not divorce him. For the unbelieving husband is sanctified by the wife, and the unbelieving wife is sanctified by the husband, otherwise, your children would be unclean, now they are clean."

I could not believe it! The Bible actually had a situation that applied to me! This is the first time that the reality of God's word being alive and pertinent to life today really stood out to me. The Bible was pertinent in my life. I did not know how something written thousands of years ago could apply to me, but it did.

Also, I Corinthians 7:15 said: "But if the unbeliever departs, let him depart; a brother or sister is not under bondage in such cases."

Ashley had also read in Sunday school a Scripture that said God hates divorce. Malachi 2:16 says, "For the Lord God of Israel says that He hates divorce, for it covers one's garment with violence." Earlier, in Malachi 2:11, the Lord refers to marriage as "the Holy institution which He loves." This chapter was talking to the children of Israel, who had taken wives who were pagans and worshipped false gods. Even in those circumstances, God said He hates divorce.

My love for God at this point in my life was starting to be my source of strength, joy, and peace. So I did not want to make another bad decision that would result in bad consequences. If God hated divorce, I did not want to initiate an action that God would hate. So I decided to stay married and pray for my husband's salvation. That seemed to be what the Scripture was telling me to do.

After making this decision and commitment to God (not my husband) to stay married and keep my vows, I ran across the book *The Power of a Praying Wife* by Stormie Omartian. I was shopping in a secular grocery store, and there it was on a shelf in the middle of the aisle. I usually never purchased anything that was not on my shopping list due to my financial situation, but I felt drawn to this book. I read through the entire book a couple times, prayed the prayers for my husband at the end of each chapter, and begged God to fix my situation.

Deep down, I wanted my husband to get saved or depart. I wanted a quick resolution to the problem. I believed with all my heart that God could save him, and he could become a new man. But I wasn't sure whether God was going to do this. I became stubborn and tenacious in my determination to obey God in relation to my marriage. My friends, who did not know God, would constantly tell me to get a divorce. Katrina would just listen and provide biblical encouragement to me. Ashley would encourage me as well, but she surprised me in hoping that the Lord would give me a divorce one day. I just assumed all Christians would look down on a divorced person. Everyone, both believing and non-believing, wanted me to be set free from my marriage. My marriage was not a good one by anyone's definition. Even in the world's eyes, my husband should have been home at night spending time with me. He should have contributed to the marriage financially and not put me in a position of being the primary breadwinner. He should have treated me with love and respect. None of this was happening. He needed to become a new person.

Another Scripture that Ashley was teaching became real to me as well. I Peter 3:1–4 says the following: "Wives, likewise, be submissive to your own husbands, that even if some do not obey the word, they, without a word, may be won by the conduct of their wives, when they observe your chaste conduct accompanied by fear. Do not let your adornment be merely outward—arranging the hair, wearing gold or putting on fine apparel—rather let it be the hidden person of the heart, with the incorruptible beauty of a gentle and quiet spirit, which is very precious in the sight of God."

There were several key concepts Ashley taught based on this Scripture. One was that the relationship between a husband and wife was unique. It tells wives to be submissive to their own husbands. It did not say be submissive to every man in the world. The spirit of submission was just as important as the act of submission. It is a joyous act in which your husband feels lifted up, respected, and important. It challenges a husband to live in obedience to God's truth. God designed man with a need for his wife to treat him in that way. God convinced me that all my complaining about my husband to our friends as a way to get through my situation was a sin. It was also harmful to me as I dwelled on my husband and his actions instead of dwelling on God and His relationship with me. When I was complaining about my situation, I was focusing my eyes on things of this world instead of the eternal things of heaven. God wanted me to focus more on Him and less on my husband. So I decided to talk about other things with my friends and pray to God about the things I thought were wrong. I actually felt better when I did not place so much attention on my situation. Some of the burden started to lift, and I felt a little freer, even though nothing had changed.

The other amazing thing I learned in relation to complaining about my husband was that, in a way, I was also complaining about myself. In Genesis, God describes marriage by saying "a man shall leave his father and mother and be joined to his wife, and they shall become one flesh." While I will not pretend to understand the intricacies of God joining two people together, it became clear to me that we were joined by God to become one flesh. This concept will be explained in further detail throughout the book.

The second primary concept that affected my life in this Scripture was the word "chaste." In 1828, Noah Webster described it as "being pure in action and language." He also described it as "being without moral defect or blemish." This convicted me to stop using bad language. This was a bad habit I had picked up in high school, where I had started saying words I had not even heard before entering the public school system. As I started to change and stopped using bad words, people started acting different around me. Even though my decision was to purify myself, people seemed to notice I did not use bad language anymore, and they seemed to use it less around me as well.

The third portion of the Scripture affected many other actions and attitudes in my life. It said that a woman could have incorruptible beauty. There is so much emphasis placed on physical beauty everywhere we turn. We see so many actresses worried about their weight and physical appearance. I spent several hours a week exercising to reduce stress and to be beautiful. But there is an *incorruptible* beauty that we can have. This beauty never dies. Have you ever met someone you thought was very attractive ... and then he or she opened his or her mouth? All of a sudden, there was no physical appeal whatsoever?

This Scripture emphasizes the opposite. Anyone can be incorruptibly beautiful through conduct. That conduct is a gentle and quiet spirit. A gentle spirit is not demanding of its rights. It is not harsh or grating. It is soothing, tranquil, soft, and peaceable. Would you rather be in a harsh and grating environment? Or would you rather be in a peaceable environment? All of these concepts were changes that occurred my heart, rather than major changes in actions. I thought that maybe through my conduct, my husband could come home to a peaceful environment and want to spend time with me. If I could truly enjoy spending time with him again, he might be drawn to God through my conduct.

At the same time that I was running full speed ahead toward God, it seemed my husband was running full speed away from Him. As quickly as I was changing into being a godly woman, he was also changing into being more of an ungodly man. We use to be in agreement about so many things. Now we could not agree on anything.

For example, a friend of ours was about forty years old and was dating someone in her early twenties. During the first year of this relationship, we would both say how gross it was. We were both surprised by a man in his late thirties being attracted to someone who was a teenager about four years older than his daughter. Later, whenever I made a comment about it, my husband would just say, "To each his own." It seemed to be such a huge age gap when we were six and a half years apart and they were twenty years apart.

Another example was that in the beginning of our marriage, we decided to allow my brother-in-law to live with us while he straightened out his life. We made a list of about twenty ground rules that would be typical for any eighteen-year-old and included items such as no loud music, no girls spending the night, no smoking, no drinking, no drugs, going to bed at a reasonable hour, etc. We put the agreement in writing, and all of us signed it.

My brother-in-law was having a hard time getting his life started on the right foot. My husband promised me that if there were any disagreements, he would always take my side, because I was his wife. As the days went on, my brother-in-law and my husband seemed to think the agreement was a joke. The dynamic of the household was that I was the outsider, even though I owned, worked on, and paid for the house. My husband continually sided with my brother-in-law over every disagreement, became increasingly irritable and secretive, started locking desk drawers, walking out of the house to talk on the phone every time it rang, and even started leaving with his brother every night instead of having a relationship with his wife.

There seemed to be nothing I could do about the situation. It felt like my hands were tied. The only thing I thought I could do was ask my husband to keep his word, and I prayed more fervently than ever that God would fix my situation. I finally told him his brother was no longer welcome in the house, and he needed to go as soon as possible. He finally moved out, and I thought I would get my life back.

Getting my brother-in-law out of the house did not fix the problem. It was too late. I was now married to a person who was very angry, irrational, withdrawn, or depressed most of the time. All his phone calls were now taking place in the yard. If his phone rang when he was home, he would go outside, even if it was pouring rain. He had new friends and acquaintances I had never met. He would run out at the drop of a hat to meet someone without telling me why. I thought, *How ridiculous can this situation get?*

I had such an internal battle over this. How could I fix this relationship? Should I tell someone who could help me? But what was the godly thing to do? I had decided to be a godly wife no matter what. I was still learning what that looked like. I knew my husband's only hope to be released from his addictions in life (smoking, pain pills, etc.) was to find the Lord. And I also knew that my only hope was for him to find the Lord, or to divorce him through biblical means. God clearly said in Malachi that He hates divorce. Jesus said that adultery is a valid reason for divorce and the person is free to remarry, and Paul said in I Corinthians 7:15 that when an unbeliever leaves that the spouse is free to remarry. Neither of these options seemed to be coming any time soon.

"In the same way, the Spirit helps us in our weakness. We do not know what we ought to pray for, but the Spirit himself intercedes for us with groans that words cannot express."— Romans 8:26

I can honestly tell you that my prayers to be rescued from this situation were prayers of desperation. I would cry myself to sleep while praying. I would pray for my husband to find God. I would pray for his deliverance from what seemed to be addictive behaviors. I would pray for a whole new life. I prayed to be rescued. The Lord just kept saying, "Trust me."

The next big thing God brought to my attention about being a godly woman was Proverbs 31. Katrina taught one Sunday for Ashley and taught this Scripture. I kept wondering why had I not heard all of these things before.

The Virtuous Wife; Proverbs 31:10–31: "Who can find a virtuous wife? For her worth is far above rubies. The heart of her husband safely trusts her; so he will have no lack of gain. She does him good and not evil all the days of her life. She seeks wool and flax, and willingly works with her hands. She is like the merchant ships, she brings her food from afar. She also rises while it is yet night, and provides food for her household, and a portion for her maidservants. She considers a field and buys it; from her profits she plants a vineyard. She girds herself with strength, and strengthens her arms. She perceives that her merchandise is good, and her lamp does not go out by night. She stretches out her hands to the distaff, and her hand holds the spindle. She extends her hand to the poor, yes, she reaches out her hands to the needy. She is not afraid of snow for her household, for all her household is clothed with scarlet. She makes tapestry for herself; her clothing is fine linen and purple. Her husband is known in the gates, when he sits among the elders of the land. She makes linen garments and sells them, and supplies sashes for the merchants. Strength and honor are her clothing; she shall rejoice in time to come. She opens her mouth with wisdom, and on her tongue is the law of kindness. She watches over the ways of her household, and does not eat the bread of idleness. Her children rise up and call her blessed; her husband also, and he praises her: 'Many daughters have done well, but you excel them all.' Charm is deceitful and beauty is passing, but a woman who fears the LORD, she shall be praised. Give her of the fruit of her hands, and let her own works praise her in the gates."

I embraced this lesson so much that I taped the Scripture to my refrigerator door and read it every day. I prayed daily for the Lord to make me into this woman. The Holy Spirit convicted me that I had to allow the Lord to change me. Proverbs31woman.com elaborated that the beauty of this passage is that it covered her character as a wife, her devotion as a homemaker, her generosity as a neighbor, her influence as a teacher, her effectiveness as a mother, and her excellence as a person. John MacArthur, Jr. further says this Proverbs was written to King Lemuel and was advice he had received from his mother regarding a godly wife. So, in aspiring to be this woman, I was aspiring to be a wife fit for a king and one any mother would want her son to have.

While I was still new in my Christian walk as an adult and was not a mother, I was convicted to have the character traits described in this passage.

Virtue

Webster's 1828 dictionary says a virtuous person was one with strength of character. A virtuous person conformed to moral and ethical principles. This concept allowed me to take some of my weaker character traits and use them for God's glory. For example, I had a tendency to be stubborn, which I inherited from my grandfather. I remember Granddaddy once changed churches because his denomination was embracing a principal that he did not consider biblical. He was head of the elders, and they just left the church. Now I could be stubborn about something good too. I could be stubborn about loving God, loving my husband, and doing what was moral and right.

Trust of her Husband

Her husband's heart could trust in her. This meant that my actions had to be those of someone my husband could trust. It did not mean he was trustworthy, only that I would be. Due to this Scripture, I turned my situation over to God. I sought God, stopped complaining about him, only talked about his good traits, did not join his parents when they started insulting him due to his not having a job, and kept many confidences. I was the only Christian he knew, and the last thing he needed was to be betrayed.

Hard Worker

She was a hard worker. She would get up early and stay up late to accomplish her responsibilities for the good of her household. I loved my sleep, so this concept was not the easiest to implement. I don't think I ever embraced getting up early, but I was motivated to work hard and accomplish all that had to be done at home and work without grumbling or complaining.

Businesswoman

She was a good businessperson who sold good merchandise. She was honest in her business dealings and was profitable in them as well. In the historical context, many business people sold items by weight using scales. They would set the scales in a way that an honest measurement wasn't given, and they would make more money. The Lord tells us we need to be honest in our business dealings. In other words, don't cheat on your time with your employer, don't steal stamps or pens from your employer, and put in an honest day's work. We should always work as unto the Lord. It is hard to work as unto the Lord as He knows all, sees all, and hears all.

Valuable Character Traits

She had character traits of strength, honor, wisdom, kindness, and compassion. In this case, wisdom is the ability to make decisions based on what is right, according to God's law. The only way to attain this kind of wisdom is spending time daily in the Scriptures to find out what is right in God's eyes.

Husband is Known in the Gates by his Wife's Actions

For some reason, the verse in which her husband is known in the gates when he sits with the elders in the land became particularly convicting for me. It meant that how I saw my husband is the way other people saw him. So I started to always try to look for the good in him. We will see at the end of this book why the Lord started to work on me now with my thoughts, deeds, and actions regarding my husband. I tried to focus on his positive character traits. If he did something I liked or made me feel good, I would compliment him on the positive qualities. I would then pray about the negative qualities and leave the rest to God.

Good Reputation

Her own works bring her praise in the gates. This means she has a good reputation. Even when you don't know it, you have a reputation. Whether it is in school, the workplace, or among your friends, you have a reputation. People will always have opinions of you. Your reputation is important, even if you try to make it unimportant and pretend it doesn't exist.

At this point in life, I was now about twenty-seven years old and had been married about a year and a half. I had been attending church regularly, praying regularly, and had started the habit of "doing quiet time." My walk with God and the level of intimacy I was building with Him was taking off like a jet airplane. We all have different phases in our walk with God. Sometimes we are moving like a turtle, other times we are walking at a steady pace, and other times we are moving at supersonic speeds. Many individuals commented about how quickly I seemed to be running toward the Lord and how passionate I was about Him.

Reading and learning about these Scriptures did not really fix my circumstances. However, God was fixing me. He was molding me just like a piece of clay into the woman He wanted me to be. Jeremiah 29:11–14a was a big encouragement to me. It says, "'For I know the plans I have for you,' says the Lord. 'They are plans for good and not for disaster, to give you a future and a hope. In those days when you pray, I will listen. If you look for me wholeheartedly, you will find me. I will be found by you,' says the Lord. 'I will end your captivity.'"

So I looked to God wholeheartedly. Even though I felt like a captive who needed freeing, I had real hope in my situation. Webster's 1828 dictionary defines hope as "confidence in a future event; the highest degree of well founded expectation of good; as a hope founded on God's gracious promises." I prayed with confidence. I would tell God, "You have promised to give me a future and a hope. You have promised me that you will listen to me. I beg you, God, to fix my situation. I don't know how to fix it, but you can fix it."

This Scripture helped me to release the things I could not control in my life, and let God control the circumstances. "Why are you cast down, O my soul? And why are you disquieted within me? Hope in God; for I shall yet praise Him, the help of my countenance and my God."—Psalm 43:5

David wrote this Psalm in times of trouble. Richard Sibbes describes it well: "You see how David's passions here are interlaced with comforts, and his comforts with passions, till at last he gets the victory of his own heart. You have some short-spirited Christians, if all be not quiet at the first, all is lost with them, but it is not so with a true Christian soul, with the best soul living."

I had an internal peace that can only be described if you experience it for yourself. The Bible calls it a peace that surpasses all understanding. It is like always being in the eye of a hurricane. Life is blowing its hardest all around you, but you have this strange stillness inside you that never seems to go away. Each day, my routine stayed the same, except I now made sure I had quiet time. I still did everything around the house and yard. I still supported a husband who did not love me and did not work. However, I did all these things with joy in my heart. I did them with a stubbornness the world did not understand. I did them with peace that God was in charge of my life. I always had that nagging desperation in the back of my mind that I wanted a godly husband. I had a deep desire for a godly husband and a spiritual leader. But there was nothing I could do to make that happen except pray. And if it did not happen, I needed to humble myself and accept it as God's will for my life.

Tim Keller, pastor of Redeemer Presbyterian Church in New York, eloquently described the situation in which I was living. In Habakkuk, Chapter 3, the whole chapter is an epilogue showing how bad things are. It talks about how bad life is for years. Verse 2 says, "In the midst of the years make it known," and verse sixteen says, "And in my place I tremble. Because I must wait quietly for the day of distress." Habakkuk was living in a situation the world would call hopeless. According to Pastor Keller, verse 17 describes a nationwide problem. There is no food as the fig tree is not blossoming and there is no fruit on the vines. There is no commerce, as a primary commerce of the area was olive oil, and they have no olives. There is no flock or cattle for food, meat, or commerce. Yet in the middle of it all, there are two gleams of hope. Verse 3 says, "His splendor covers the heavens, and the earth is full of His praise." Verse 18 says, "Yet I will exult in the Lord, I will rejoice in the God of my salvation. The Lord God is my strength."

Pastor Keller went on to explain that to rejoice in the God of my salvation was to treasure, savor, or adore God. "Rejoice" does not mean to be happy, because we can't just be happy in terrible circumstances. But we can treasure God; we can adore God, even when our circumstances fail. My life at this point felt as hopeless as Habakkuk's. Yet I was rejoicing in the God of my salvation. There was no end in sight to my circumstance, and the promise I made to God was to stay in this marriage for the rest of my life. But even when love failed me, I could treasure God and what He had done for me.

Johnna's story

Johnna was the mom of two beautiful children. Her husband loved her very much. Johnna took the children to church every week by herself. She had a secret that few knew about. Her husband was an alcoholic. He was the greatest husband in the world as long as he was not drinking.

One day, Johnna could not stand it any longer, and she prayed to God, "I don't care what you do to me, but please, save my husband and release him from his addiction to alcohol."

Johnna told her husband about her prayer. About six weeks later, Johnna unexpectedly went into the hospital with a life-threatening illness. She was in a coma for two weeks. Her husband prayed for her to be healed, and the Lord listened. She was healed with no explanation of what caused her illness. Her husband came to know the Lord, and is now a recovering alcoholic. Johnna had the faith to release control of her earthly circumstances to the Lord for her husband's salvation.

I would receive much advice to leave the marriage. I would also receive encouragement from Christian ladies regarding my tenacity to follow God's will no matter where He led me. Some Christian ladies would say, "I don't know how you do it. Are you sure God wants you in this situation?" Others would say how much of an encouragement it was to them to see me coming to church each week, and that it motivated them to keep coming. It made them want to be closer to God as well. All I knew was that the only way I was going to survive this situation was to be close to God. I didn't realize people were watching me and considering me a leader at this point. I had only recently started providing input during Sunday school when questions were asked. Previously, I was just a sponge trying to absorb what I could from the teaching. Then the emotional roller-coaster really started to get going.

Chapter 3
Waiting on God

I like to be in control of my life. Yet my circumstances were making it impossible for me to have any resemblance of a normal marriage. Many times I wanted to take action to fix my situation. I could do it my way, or I could do it God's way. I could not discern whether my leading to take action was from God or from the world.

My pastor, Steven Smith, once said that if you aren't sure about the path God is leading you on, you wait. He called this "actively waiting." You pray and wait for God to lead you in a particular direction. It is active waiting because God has a plan and is working, even if you don't think anything is happening. This was the Lord showing me it was okay for Him to be in control, and not me. The Scriptures that the Lord showed me in this situation all confirmed that I should not take any action.

"Be still and know that I am God."—Psalm 46:10a. So what does it mean to be still and know that God is God? First, you have to be still. There are various ways to do this. The way that worked best for me was to first listen to Christian music that focused on God's glory. Some of my favorite musicians were Casting Crowns, Third Day, Mercy Me, and Ray Boltz. I spent a few minutes each day listening to and reflecting on their music. Then I read a daily devotional. Then I wrote something down. It started out that I would only write a verse that had particular meaning to me that day when I was reading. Or I would write down the date and a sentence that had meaning to me. My experience in journaling is that when I write, my brain slows down. I can stop and listen to what God is saying, because I am completely focused on hearing and thinking about the word of God. For me, writing something down was the trick to learn how to "be still." It was at those moments that I started to really know God. I wasn't focused on my circumstances. I was focused on God, and it brought me great joy for just a few minutes.

"Wait for the LORD; be strong and take heart and wait for the LORD."—Psalm 27:14

"Yet those who wait for the LORD will gain new strength; they will mount up with wings like eagles, they will run and not get tired, they will walk and not become weary."—Isaiah 40:31

This pair of Scriptures told me to wait for the Lord—to be strong and wait for the Lord. The words "be strong" were wrapped by the words "wait for the Lord." Again, I felt like God was saying, "Just trust me. Get your strength from me. Now is the time to just wait."

Then Isaiah 40:31 again said to wait for the Lord. If you wait for the Lord, you will get strength. Have you ever tried to run a long distance? My daily life felt like I was in this never-ending marathon. I am not a long distance runner by any stretch of the imagination, so I felt weary quite often. I longed to be able to run and not get tired. This verse told me that if I waited for the Lord, I would be able to run the race of life and not get tired. As I continued to wait, I continued to run or walk the race of life, and I started to not get tired. The more joy, patience, and contentment I found with God, the more fiery darts would come my way. Ephesians 6:12 tells us that we do not wrestle with flesh and blood, but against principalities, against powers, against the rulers of the darkness of this age, against spiritual hosts of wickedness in the heavenly places. Occasionally I would have a great evening with my husband. We would eat dinner together and watch a movie. We would have nice conversation and talk about our direction in life. I would get hope, and then the next day, things would return to normal. He would talk about how unhappy he was, and I would be so disappointed that I was living my life in circles.

The spiritual attacks just kept getting stronger. My husband was the primary person who would go into this huge depressive state. Since we were one flesh, it would affect me. Instead of saying he wasn't happy, he would say, I don't love you anymore. My friends would tell me how horrible my marriage was and how wrong I was for not ending it. I would have horrible, internal thoughts about my ability to trust God or the Bible and make right decisions. This is when I knew the Spiritual attacks and darts would be coming from every direction. John 1:5 tells us that "the light shines in the darkness, and the darkness did not overcome it." Jesus was the light of the world John was referring to. Circumstances made me feel like I was in darkness much of the time. But, John says, darkness cannot overcome the light. It is encouraging to think that Christ is our light. And no matter how bright or how dim, darkness is never able to overcome light. The light of Christ always shines.

I wanted to feel empowered, and the only way to do this was to depend on Christ. My husband showed signs of being manic depressive and was not happy in the world. I would get depressed, doubt myself, run to God and find strength, and the cycle started over. But eventually, I just got used to the attacks. I was growing closer to the Lord, and I didn't become emotional so much. I would put up my shield of faith and let the Lord take over the situation. This was one of my first steps toward freedom. I learned that my thoughts and emotions did not have to be same as my husband's thoughts and emotions. The reality was that I had made my husband and relationships idols in my life that the Lord needed to remove for me.

You would think with all I was doing to obey God, my circumstances would have improved. I kept thinking my husband was going to find hope in Christ any day now. Days turned into weeks, and weeks turned into months. It seemed like an eternity. Little did I know at the time that God had a lot of molding left to do in me. Have you ever watched a clay cup or bowl being molded into the perfect shape to hold water? It starts out as a big glob. The potter turns the wheel and squeezes with firm hands until the clay starts to soften and mold. The more the wheel turns, the more pliable the clay becomes. Layer by layer, the potter continues to work the clay into the perfect shape. At this point in my life, I believed God was just getting started. He had a lot more layers to work through before I would start to resemble any recognizable shape. I was beginning to learn that obedience and submission to God is a good thing.

But my circumstances only seemed to worsen. God almost never does things the way we think He is going to do them, and certainly not in our own timeframe. The inevitable finally happened. One Wednesday, I was driving home from work. I turned my car into my driveway and found my husband at home. His best friend's work truck was also in the driveway. As soon as I turned the corner, I thought, *He is going to leave me.* While I desperately wanted my situation to change, I was not prepared for this. I thought we had left all this emotional game playing in our relationship back in high school. Here I was again. We had made a commitment and promise to God to love each other for the rest of our lives, but it seems I was the only one who really wanted to honor my promise to God. He just went through the motions.

I pulled into the driveway, and his best friend walked out of my house, got into his white work van, and left without saying a word to me. This was highly unusual as we were also good friends. Then I went inside the house. My husband sat me down at the kitchen table and sat across from me.

He said, "I'm not happy."

As I stared through him toward my back yard, I said, "Who is?"

He said, "One of the perks of my new job is that I accepted an apartment they are offering me and I am moving out tonight."

I said, "Do what you have to do," and I left. I went to the house of a friend of mine for a few hours while he gathered his stuff and left. The funny thing is, all he really took was his clothes, because everything else in the house was mine. He left his tools and broken down cars in the yard to pick up at a later date.

I was devastated. I cried all night. I might have gotten two hours' sleep. I was several hours late to work as I tried to pull myself together. I felt like I was in mourning. I wanted to be free, I wanted a different circumstance, but I did not want to be divorced. I thought God was going to save my husband and change him. Matthew 5:4 says, "Blessed are those who mourn, for they shall be comforted." I needed to be comforted. It felt like someone had died. I had lost half of my being. I wasn't feeling very blessed, but I was feeling closer and more dependent on God. This Greek word in

Matthew for "mourn" is the strongest word for mourning in the language. It is for the mourning of the dead. To mourn is to care deeply,... to know the meaning of suffering because of the sin, injustice, and perversion in society. Jesus assures us that those who mourn will receive the comfort of God, for in this realism one draws near to God and God in turn draws near to him. God was all I had in this moment in time. The Holy Spirit was my comforter.

My parents sent my pastor's wife, Ashley, to comfort me, and I will never forget what she said: "The Bible says God will be a husband to the husbandless." She prayed with me and left. I mourned this day more than I mourned the passing of my grandmother, who had died the previous year. It felt like someone had ripped off my arms and my legs without using anesthesia. I now knew what the Bible meant when it says that two shall become one. It seemed like half of me was gone.

Now it was time to recover. I gathered strength from all the verses I had learned, and allowed God to comfort me. I got dressed and went to work. I felt humiliated. I knew God wanted to give me a future and a hope. I had to let my husband go, because he was an unbeliever, and that is what the Bible told me to do. I was convinced now more than ever that the Lord was not going to save him. The Lord was going to help me run without growing weary. Each day started to get a little easier. My quiet times were hours at a time in my living room instead of a few minutes with my door closed in my bedroom, hoping my husband would not disturb me if he came home. The truth of my life became that I was now a separated, Christian woman. My marriage had been a failure. No matter how much I tried to show love to my husband, the love had not been returned. My husband had abandoned our marriage because he was not happy.

John 1:12, 14 and 16 says, "But as many as received Him, to them He gave the right to become children of God, to those who believe in His name: And the Word became flesh and dwelt among us, and we beheld His glory, the glory of the only begotten of the Father, full of grace and truth. And of His fullness we have all received, and grace for grace."

I was now on my way to having an even more intimate relationship with the God of the universe. This was the beginning of a long road of learning what Scripture meant when it says we receive grace for grace. It means that no matter what our circumstances, the Lord continues to provide grace. We live our lives so empty much of the time. But Christ came, and He was full of grace and truth. My new truth of the circumstances in my life was overwhelming and embarrassing to me. But, the truth that I was a child of God gave me strength to get up each morning. The truth, that God became man and suffered life in this world just as I did, helped me to take in a breath each day. It gave me the strength to get up, go to work, and face the world when all I wanted to do, all I had the inner strength to do, was hide under the covers. And this grace and truth was endless from Christ, was endless for all eternity. Grace piled upon grace kept coming to me.

I started gaining some emotional strength and started the healing process. Then it happened. Within a week, I receive a phone call from my husband that he wanted to work things out. So he came over and said he loves and misses me. He said he wanted to go to church with me, that he left me because I was doing everything around the house without complaining, and he felt guilty. He did not understand my motives in trying to make the house so welcoming to him. But he still loved me. The most encouraging part of this conversation was that my husband was actually noticing all that God was doing in me. My chaste and quiet spirit was making an impact. My desire to be a Proverbs 31 woman was impacting him whether he knew it or not.

I was also confused. I'm supposed to let an unbeliever go when he leaves, but what do I do when he comes back? There was not a clear answer in Scripture for me. The excitement about my future turned into anticipation. I thought God was releasing me from my mistakes, but He wasn't. I now had to search the Scriptures to figure out what to do.

Here are the Scriptures the Lord kept bringing me back to:

> "For if you forgive men their trespasses, your heavenly Father will also forgive you. But if you do not forgive men their trespasses, neither will your Father forgive your trespasses."— Matthew 6:14–15

> "Then Peter came to Him and said, 'Lord, how often shall my brother sin against me, and I forgive him? Up to seven times?'

Jesus said to him, 'I do not say to you, up to seven times, but up to seventy times seven.'"—Matthew 18:21–22

So what do you do when an unbeliever comes back? I searched the Scriptures. The Lord seemed to think the next thing I really needed to learn was what it was like to live in continual forgiveness. My personality was such that I could get mad and not talk to someone for days. But that was not a Christ-like characteristic. So I had to make the decision to forgive, and have blind trust that the Lord knew what He was doing. I had to trust that His intentions toward me were to work things out for my good. So I did the only thing I could. I decided to forgive my husband and give him the opportunity to come to church with me and meet Jesus.

He did not move back in right away. He came to church one Sunday and invited me to come visit him at his apartment.

I said, "I am an adult woman, and we are married. This is our home. If you want to come to church with me and move back in the house, then do it. But there was no way I am going to visit you at an apartment."

So he moved back in. The agreement was that he would go at least every other week to church. Weeks and months passed as I reminded him of his promise. He came to church with me one time, and that was it. I still had to honor my decision to be his wife, because I was honoring God. However, he rarely kept any of his promises to me.

I was still mentally in a place where I was starting to heal from him leaving the relationship in the first place. Now I was also adjusting to him being back in the house. Though he was physically in the house, I was mentally and spiritually torn from him. His leaving had created so much scar tissue that I was just going through the motions to be his wife. I spent more time at the gym, unless he asked me not to go. I started more of my own hobbies, such as gardening and doing things I could do on my own. If he asked, I would put him first, as the Bible commanded. He rarely asked, and we never went on a date. I got involved in more church activities and picnics. But if he was out doing his own thing, that was fine too, as I had the space to spend time with God.

When he moved out of the house, my friend Katrina told me about a Christian singles group in the area. I started watching their website from a distance. I had made the comment to her that I did not know where I was going to find friends who had similar interests. I enjoyed being outdoors, going to the beach, and was a very active person. Katrina told me about the site and how many friends she had who were a part of the group. I wasn't really looking to date at this point. I was just looking for female friends and activities. I started monitoring the group's activities on the web. I felt like I could not participate since I was in this crazy situation, but it gave me hope that I could make some more Christian friends at some point in the future.

While I was monitoring this group from a distance, God was also teaching me that I looked to earthly things too much for my contentment. By making me wait to build new relationships, He was teaching me that everything on this Earth, including relationships, are all temporary and nothing can fill the void I had inside me, except God. If I looked to anything besides God for contentment, I was looking at an idol. God taught me that I should not hold on to anything too strongly, or He might take it away. The only thing I needed to hold on to was God. Anything else, whether it be money, relationships, friendships, looks, or anything else, would never provide contentment. My desires and my focus on earthly things was slowly dying.

I was in a strange place in my life. I was becoming a strong individual who was married and honored her wedding vows. I honored those vows because I had made a promise to God. Yet I also was no longer feeling quite so trapped by those vows. It was freeing to honor those vows to God and not think of it as honoring my husband. I was at a point where I did not really need him, because I had God. That actually made me a better wife, as my happiness and contentment did not rest on his shoulders. He was free to be an individual without worrying about how his actions affected me.

I also felt free from my husband. If my husband was in a bad mood, which was usually the case, I let him be in a bad mood. I would pray and let God handle it. I felt like my desires in life were dying. I felt like I was experiencing a slow death. Yet there was an uncanny freedom in that death that freed me to just let the world pass me by and keep my focus on God. I was starting to gain an understanding of what it meant to be an alien and sojourner in this world.

This theme is repeated over and over in Scripture from Abraham in Genesis to many chapters in the New Testament:

> "For our citizenship is in heaven, from which we also eagerly wait for the Savior, the Lord Jesus Christ."—Philippians 3:20
>
> "Beloved, I urge you as sojourners and pilgrims, abstain from fleshly lusts which war against the soul."—1 Peter 2:11
>
> "I am a stranger in the earth."—Ephesians 2:19
>
> "All these died in faith, without receiving the promises, but having seen them and having welcomed them from a distance, and having confessed that they were strangers and exiles on Earth.... But as it is, they desire a better country, that is, a heavenly one."—Hebrews 11:13, 16a

Things of this Earth really started to have little value to me. I felt like a stranger on this planet in every way. It was like being a visitor to a foreign country or someone else's family. You observe their traditions, and you may even participate, but you don't really grasp them as if it was your own family. It is like living in a foreign country on a permanent basis; you never really feel like you are at home. I had been in this situation so long and had so much scar tissue from the emotional injuries that it felt like my earthly spirit and desires had died and were still dying inside me.

I started to change in many ways during the first year that followed his first move out of the house. I did my quiet time with my door open whether my husband was home or not. I shared my contentment with God, and talked about what I was learning. I no longer hid my joy from God in my own house. I was hoping my insights would give my husband a desire for this unexplained contentment that he was so desperately looking for in life. I was finding out that contentment was so much better than happiness.

Webster's defines "contented" as "satisfied, quiet; easy in mind." It goes on to say, "It is our duty to be contented with the dispensations of providence." This means we should be satisfied with the hand God has dealt to us. John Piper says "God is most glorified in us when we are most satisfied in Him." I like to use Webster's 1828 dictionary, as it has Bible verses and biblical definitions of English words. Our modern dictionaries have taken God out of the English language.

If you have ever wondered if God looks out for his children while they are on earth, keep reading. One of the things that God has assured me of over the past few years is that He is the same yesterday, today and forever.

In the following verse, David is talking to King Saul, who is trying to kill him. "Let the Lord judge between you and me, and let the Lord avenge me on you. But my hand shall not be against you. As the proverb of the ancients says, Wickedness proceeds from the wicked. But my hand shall not be against you. After whom has the king of Israel come out? Whom do you pursue? A dead dog? A flea? Therefore, let the Lord be judge, and judge between you and me, and see and plead my case, and deliver me out of your hand."—I Samuel 24:12–15

Within a couple of weeks of moving back into the house, my husband broke out in the worst case of shingles (adult chicken pox, essentially; a condition where you break out in a very painful rash) his doctor had ever seen. They gave him medicine, but he kept breaking out. The entire right side of his torso (front and back) and entire right arm were covered. He stayed like this for two months. Finally, he sat me down at the kitchen table and said he kept getting the advice that the truth will set him free. He was visibly nervous. I was wondering what else he could possibly have to tell me. The last time he sat me down at the kitchen table, it was to tell me he was moving out of the house. So he proceeded to tell me that while he was living in the apartment, he'd had a one-night stand. He told me he had not talked to the person since and that he would be faithful from here on out. His shingles were gone within a week.

I passionately believe God looks out for those who are faithful to Him. He did it thousands of years ago, and He does it today. The Lord avenged me in ways I could have never avenged myself, and God does a better job than we can.

I now had two solid reasons to end this marriage. One was that my unbelieving husband had left, and the other was that he had been unfaithful. In both instances, the Bible says I would be free to remarry. But what did God want me to do?

I read the book called *Tough Love* by Dr. James C. Dobson. It was written to help Christian couples overcome adultery in their marriage. My limitation was that "we" were not a Christian couple. However, the principles in the book sounded biblical to me. I did not feel freedom to leave the marriage due to a one-night stand, especially since he was asking for my forgiveness and was living in the house again. So, again, I decided to forgive him. I implemented the principles in the book, such as setting boundaries and expectations. However, these actions were all one-sided. The more boundaries and expectations he agreed to, the more he emotionally closed down from the marriage.

Moreover, I began to wonder why he had even moved back into the house. He again quit his job, and I was again supporting him. Days turned into weeks, and weeks turned into months. There was always a good excuse for him not to work at a particular job. The relationship remained one-sided. I still supported us financially, physically, and emotionally. I still did everything around the house. I still was the only one making an attempt at showing love. I started to feel like I was losing myself each day. Through stubborn determination I stayed in the marriage until I got some other instruction from the Lord. But it felt like there was a price to be paid.

I was living Matthew 16:24–26: "Then Jesus said to His disciples, 'If anyone desires to come after Me, let him deny himself, and take up his cross, and follow Me. For whoever desires to save his life will lose it, but whoever loses his life for My sake will find it. For what profit is it to a man if he gains the whole world, and loses his own soul? Or what will a man give in exchange for his soul?'"

Each day, I felt like I was living this verse. My desires to move forward in life with a godly husband were put on a back burner. I felt like I continued to whither each day. It was like I was being torn apart piece by piece. The Lord was teaching me to hold on to Him, not hold on to anything of this Earth. A small voice was whispering in my head that Jesus denied himself by dying on the cross for me. His flesh died even though He had never sinned. I felt like I was doing the same. All Jesus was asking me to do was stay in marriage I had originally chosen. Staying in the marriage made me utterly dependent on Him to function each day. As I struggled through this slow, emotional death, I battled anxiety, hopelessness, and depression. But my true hope was that in the end, I would gain my life in heaven. The funny thing was, as my earthly flesh and spirit died, my heavenly spirit had more room to grow and live. Eventually, I had more of my heavenly spirit than fleshly spirit inside me. I continually felt more freedom from this Earth than I even thought possible.

It was at this point in my life, about two and a half years into the marriage, that the Lord started to really teach me how much He loved me. I started to gain an understanding of what God's love for us really was. God's love was a one-sided promise that God made to us over and over and over again. God made that promise to Abraham, telling Abraham he would be the father of many nations. God made this promise and kept it whether Abraham was faithful or not.

God also made a promise to David, that through his heir, God's kingdom would be established forever: "When your days are fulfilled and you rest with your fathers, I will set up your seed after you, who will come from your body, and I will establish his kingdom. He shall build a house for My name, and I will establish the throne of his kingdom forever. I will be his Father, and he shall be My son. If he commits iniquity, I will chasten him with the rod of men and with the blows of the sons of men. But My mercy shall not depart from him, as I took it from Saul, whom I removed from before you. And your house and your kingdom shall be established forever before you. Your throne shall be established forever."—II Samuel 7:12-16

However, David made a huge mess out of his life. He had several wives. He committed adultery and got another man's wife pregnant. Then, to hide his adultery, he had that man killed in battle. God struck the baby ill as a result of the adultery, and it died. David made such a mess of his life that all his children were untimely killed, except Solomon. Solomon was born to the wife David gained through the adultery, and then later, Jesus was born as David's heir through Solomon. God kept his promise, even when David seemed to make every mistake he could have made. He broke every commandment, yet David was still referred to as a man after God's own heart.

The encouragement I gained from this story is that God is so patient and so very faithful to us. Even though I made a huge mess out of my life, God was being faithful to me. He could still use me for His kingdom purpose, even though my actions had made a mess. He still had a lot of things to teach me, but at least now I was listening.

It was time to wait on the Lord again. I did not have a clear direction from the Lord what I should do, other than to stay married. I had to let the circumstances of life continue to move forward while I waited on the Lord to give me direction. There are so many stories in the Bible of God making promises to people, and then they had to wait.

In Acts 7:25, we see that Moses knew at the age of approximately forty that the call on his life was to deliver his people from the Egyptians. However, the people did not recognize God's call on Moses' life, so he fled, and spent forty years in the desert tending sheep and raising a family. Then God spoke through a burning bush, and it was time for Moses to actually deliver his people from slavery.

In 1 Samuel 16, as a young boy, David was anointed king of Israel. He had many events in his life that prepared him to be king. He played the harp to calm King Saul that allowed him the opportunity to observe the responsibilities of a king. He went to battle for King Saul, which gave him the experience he needed as a warrior. He waited about twenty-five years to actually become king.

Hannah prayed year after year to have a child. She wept bitterly before the Lord and was accused by the priest of being drunk because she was so intently begging the Lord for a child. Hannah became Samuel's mother, but only after years of waiting to have a child (I Samuel 1).

Elizabeth had to wait until she was well advanced in years to have a baby (Luke 1:1–25). Many estimate she was about eighty when she became the mother of John the Baptist.

Paul attempted to enter into Christian ministry after his conversion on the road to Damascus (Acts 9:1–19). However, his reputation of being a persecutor of Christians preceded him. He had to run away to Arabia for three years after conversion before attempting to make further contact with Jesus' disciples (Acts 9:26 and Galatians 1:11–19). Paul testifies in his letter to the Galatians that during these three years, Jesus continued to reveal Himself to Paul, and only after these three years did the disciples finally accept Paul. After being accepted by the disciples, he is sent home for another four years. Finally, after seven years, Paul gets to go into Christian ministry with the disciples. All of this is to say the Christian life is a process of growing and waiting (Galatians 1:20–2:1).

After seeing that God's timing is not the same as mine, I waited. In every circumstance in the Bible, the Lord was working in individuals' lives even when they did not know or expect it. He was building character and working all things for their good even though they just felt like they were struggling each and every day.

Being an only child, I never really had to learn much about forgiveness, but the Lord was going to be teaching me a lot. This was a daily decision for me as my feelings did not support the need for forgiveness. I was very hurt. I decided my husband's salvation was more important than my temporary happiness on Earth. I did not feel like forgiving him. I was not happy about the situation. I *decided* to forgive him for leaving the marriage. From this point forward, my love for him was a decision, not a feeling.

Chapter 4
Love

There are many things the world teaches us about love. It teaches us that love is a feeling, an attraction, a bond with someone. It teaches us that love is good as long as it works in our favor. There are countless songs about love, such as "Love Makes the World Go 'Round" or "All We Need is Love."

However, when the feeling stops, you are not in love any more, not with that person, anyway. The world's view of love is self-centered. The world teaches us that if we no longer feel that attraction, the person we are with must not be our "soul mate." Dictionary.com says that love is "a profoundly tender, passionate affection for another person." Another definition of love on dictionary.com says that love is the act of having sex.

In 1828, Webster's dictionary defined love as an affection of the mind excited by beauty and worth of any kind. It went on to say that love is opposed to hatred. Love between the sexes is a compound affection, consisting of esteem, benevolence, and animal desire. Love is ardent friendship or a strong attachment springing from goodwill and esteem. The love of God is the first duty of man, and this springs from just views of his attributes or excellencies of character, which afford the highest delight to the sanctified heart.

The Bible also has much to say about love. John 3:16 is one of the most popular verses quoted.

"For God so loved the world, that He gave His only begotten Son, that whosoever believes in Him shall not perish, but have eternal life." John 3:16

If the world's current view of love were true, what did Christ's dying for us accomplish? What advantage to God was there to give me His Son? What advantage to God was there in giving you His son? What affection could God have had toward us – his enemies (Romans 5:10)? Would any affection for an enemy have overshadowed his affection for His own Son? Love must mean something else besides the world's current definition.

"Know therefore that the LORD your God, He is God, the faithful God, who keeps His covenant and His loving kindness to a thousandth generation with those who love Him and keep His commandments."—Deuteronomy 7:9

"For I am convinced that neither death, nor life, nor angels, nor principalities, nor things present, nor things to come, nor powers, nor height, nor depth, nor any other created thing, will be able to separate us from the love of God, which is in Christ Jesus our Lord."—Romans 8:38–39

I am studying these verses in a marriage where my husband has left me, has come back, and has admitted to having a one-night stand while he was not living in my house, and I decided to forgive him. Now God wanted me to learn what love is. God was not only teaching me about love, He was teaching me how to love. And He was taking the blinders off my eyes as to how much He loved me. Every lesson I learned about love in this marriage was a lesson God was teaching me about Himself and His character as well. These things that God was teaching me really humbled me into being grateful to have started a love relationship with the all-powerful God of the universe.

The first character trait of love that God really brought to my attention in these verses is that love is faithful. I had made a promise to love God and keep his commandments as a child when I asked Him to become part of my life. Yet I was not capable of keeping His commandments. This meant I was not capable of being faithful to Him. I did not understand it meant turning my back on worldly things. I did not understand that it meant being obedient to God's word even when it was not the popular thing to do. I spent years trying to do things my way, and God was faithful to me the entire time. I was in this situation because that is what I wanted. I wanted to date the person I dated, and I wasn't really willing to hear any advice to the contrary.

Now, twelve years later, God is showing me how faithful He is. God was faithful to me even when I wasn't faithful to Him. God was so faithful, He had his Son go through a gruesome death for me knowing I was not going to remain faithful to Him for many years of my life. I ignored Him, and He still remained faithful.

In order for me to fully understand what that meant, God put me in a position to be faithful to someone who was not faithful to me. My husband cheated on me. He turned his back on me. He did not really want me in his life. Yet I remained faithful to him. I continued to try to be the best wife I could. I continued to try to allow God's love to flow through me so he could have a glimpse of how awesome God was. For years, I remained faithful to loving someone who really did not love me. And that is what God does for us every day of our lives. Yet He does it perfectly.

I had many realizations that hit home during this period of my life. My first realization was that I had sinned greatly by putting myself in this situation. Had I obeyed God, I never would have ended up in this situation. The sin that is causing me so much pain was the result of sin that also caused God pain. God's commandments were there to protect me, not to keep me from enjoying life. They were written by the God who created me and knows me better than I know myself. God knows the damage sin can cause even when it is something we bring upon ourselves.

My second realization was that I needed to confess my sins to God. This was the first time I felt true humility in relation to my sin. This was the first time in my life that I felt small—like my portion of the world really did not revolve around me. It was the first time in my life I felt deep down in my heart that I was a sinner who really needed God's forgiveness. Most of my life, I had a knowledge that I needed my sins forgiven. I was thankful to be going to heaven and that Jesus had died for me. But this time, I had more of a deep down regret in my heart and felt I needed God's individual forgiveness. I did not just need to know He died for my sin and the world's sin, but I needed to embrace the forgiveness I was receiving for my individual sin.

My third realization was that Jesus had suffered greatly on the cross, and it was my individual sin that put Him there. I always had a picture of Jesus on the cross for the sins of the world. Now I had more of a picture that I put Him there. Before Jesus even went to the cross for me, He knew how my life would turn out. He knew the depth of my sin. He knew the depth of my pride and arrogance that would need to be molded. He gave up living in heaven, was born into this world, and died on the cross for me. Do you know anyone who would do that for you besides Jesus?

My actions as a result of these realizations included confession, prayer, and deepened quiet times. I felt great remorse, freedom, and gratefulness at the same time. The Lord gave me a renewed spirit. I discovered a feeling of inner freedom that comes from confessing your shortcomings to God. I challenge you to ask the Holy Spirit to bring to your attention the sin in your life and confess them to God. You will be glad you did, because God has compassion on us and hurls our sins into the depths of the sea (Micah 7:18–19). This discovery also gave me the strength and motivation to remain faithful to my marriage. God was not asking me to die on a cross for my husband. God was asking me to show His love to my husband even when I did not have any love of my own to share. After what God had done for me, I felt challenged and strengthened to do this for my husband.

The other key concept I focused on from this verse is that love is kind. There are many examples of kindness in the Bible. The most famous is probably the story of the Good Samaritan. A man is beaten and left dead on the road. A stranger from a different town and is of a different ethnic background comes along. He takes care of the man left for dead on the road. He even uses his own money to pay for the man's care. It wasn't convenient to stop everything he was doing to help this man, but he did it anyway. The act of kindness is very close to the concept of grace. In today's terms, kindness is seeing someone else's need and meeting it without expecting anything in return. It is also a demeanor or character trait. Do you have a demeanor that offers a kind word to others? Or is your demeanor grumpy all the time? A kind demeanor offers encouraging words even when you don't feel like it and they are not deserved.

God is being overwhelmingly kind to this world even though it is not deserved. This world is full of sin. God spoke the world into existence and could just as easily speak it out of existence. His work is not done yet, and all have not heard or experienced God. My responsibility was to show kindness to my husband, which is nothing more than a character trait of God's love flowing through me.

The next realization that God showed me about love is found in Galatians 2:20: "I have been crucified with Christ; and it is no longer I who live, but Christ lives in me; and the life which I now live in the flesh I live by faith in the Son of God, who loved me and gave Himself up for me."

The realization was that love had to be willing. Even though I still did not feel like loving my husband, I had to be willing to. Love is not something you can fake. Love is so selfless that you put the other person above yourself. When Christ came and died on the cross, He put my need for forgiveness above His own need not to be crucified. Christ was willingly crucified for me.

Galatians reminded me that I am now "crucified" with Christ. This means that the part of me that would choose not to love my husband needs to be crucified, or killed. The part of me that chooses to sin is nailed to a cross. And instead of that part of me continuing to make decisions on my behalf, I now have Christ, who can make better decisions on my behalf, living in me. The world would still tell me to leave my husband, to not love my husband, and to not be faithful to him. However, since Christ is living in me and He gave Himself up for me, it is my turn to do the same for my husband until the Lord tells me otherwise. Each day, I felt as though I was giving up a portion of myself to decide to love my husband. It felt like I was being crucified each day. I had to love someone who did not love me in return. Yet this was another way God was showing me a small portion of His side of His relationship with me.

This taught me that love is selfless. You put the other person's needs or desires ahead of your own. Love is humble. Love is the action of pouring oneself into another person to make their lives better. That is what God does for us through the Holy Spirit each day. He lives in us. He has poured Himself into us to make us better … to make our lives better. It is impossible for us to perfectly make another person's life better, but God perfectly makes our lives better one step at a time.

The most beautiful concept about God that hit me through this process is found in 1 John. The Scripture tells us that "God is love." The times I had these various realizations about God and His character, I really felt the Holy Spirit living and growing inside me. It was such an awesome feeling. Then it brought such peace and joy to meditate and think about being in the presence of God. He is love. He is perfect love. He is perfect peace. He is all-powerful, and He is all-knowing. As a result, He commands us to love one another. If we love one another, then we know God. After all I had been going through, including the choice to love my husband, I felt I knew God better than I had ever known Him before. It was an intimate knowledge and appreciation of God.

"Beloved, let us love one another, for love is from God; and everyone who loves is born of God and knows God. The one who does not love does not know God, for God is love. By this the love of God was manifested in us, that God has sent His only begotten Son into the world so that we might live through Him. In this is love, not that we loved God, but that He loved us and sent His Son to be the propitiation for our sins. Beloved, if God so loved us, we also ought to love one another. No one has seen God at any time; if we love one another, God abides in us, and His love is perfected in us. By this we know that we abide in Him and He in us, because He has given us of His Spirit. We have seen and testify that the Father has sent the Son to be the Savior of the world. Whoever confesses that Jesus is the Son of God, God abides in him, and he in God. We have come to know and have believed the love which God has for us God is love, and the one who abides in love abides in God, and God abides in him. By this, love is perfected with us, so that we may have confidence in the day of judgment; because as He is, so also are we in this world. There is no fear in love; but perfect love casts out fear, because fear involves punishment, and the one who fears is not perfected in love. We love, because He first loved us. If someone says, 'I love God' and hates his brother, he is a liar; for the one who does not love his brother whom he has seen, cannot love God whom he has not seen."—I John 4:7–21

Have you ever thought about the word "manifest"? Webster's defined it in 1828 as "plain, open, and clearly visible to the eye; detected." God's love is clearly visible to us when we claim the gift of His Son to be our replacement on the cross. His love is detected through this gift. Anyone who confesses Jesus as the Son of God and looks to Him for salvation has God abiding in him and him in God. This means that God dwells in us, and we dwell with God. Have you ever thought about dwelling with God? That thought brings me immeasurable joy. This joy should cause our lives to be different. The love we have for the world, as a result, should cause the world to detect Christ in us. We have the Holy Spirit living in us. We should have lives full of inner strength, confidence, and an inexplicable love because God is living in and through us in every situation.

My grandfather recently passed away, and while I miss him greatly, I am also somewhat jealous that he is in the presence of God. I kept thinking about the song "I can Only Imagine" by Mercy Me. Right now, I personally can only imagine how I will react in God's presence. Will I stand? Will I fall? Will I be able to speak? I don't think any of us can know how we will react, but my granddaddy knows and is in the presence of perfect love. He is abiding with God for eternity.

"But just as it is written, 'Things which eye has not seen and ear has not heard, and which have not entered the heart of man, all that God has prepared for those who love Him.'"—I Corinthians 2:9

What this is telling us is that it is beyond our wildest imagination how wonderful heaven is going to be. I have experienced only a glimpse of God's presence in my walk with Him, and it has given me internal peace that most individuals cannot understand.

All of my realizations regarding God's love took place during approximately another year of marriage. I was now in my third year. This past year seemed like an eternity, but I was actually grateful for what God was teaching me. He taught me about Himself and how to be a reflection of Him in this world. He was continually teaching me how wrong the world's wisdom is, and He was molding me into a beautiful new woman who could reflect His love to the world. He was taking my stubborn personality traits and turning them into something good that could bring glory to God. He was teaching me not to hate, because it is not a reflection of God in this world. He was instilling in my life a purpose to be an ambassador for Christ to a lost world. We are to be salt, which prevents decay, and light, which destroys darkness.

I was now at a place in my life where I deeply desired a godly husband in every part of my being. However, my desire not to sin was stronger than my desire to take action without God's leading. I had two themes for this year of my life. One was that if I could be a godly wife to an ungodly husband, then I could say with confidence that I could be a godly wife to a godly husband if God ever gave me that opportunity. The second was that I now had a small understanding of how painful it was for God to make such sacrifices to show His love for me, even though I constantly rejected Him.

Chapter 5

Desires of Your Heart

Now I started wanting things I had never really wanted before. There were some deep desires in my heart of things I just had not thought possible. I had the desire to tithe, but I was deeply in debt. I had the desire to submit to a godly husband, but my husband was not godly and really wanted nothing to do with me. I had the desire to have two children by the age of thirty-five. I was now twenty-nine and in a marriage where we agreed to never have children. Why was it that I was changing so much?

Psalms 37:3–5 tells us, "Trust in the Lord, and do good; dwell in the land, and feed on His faithfulness. Delight yourself also in the Lord, and He shall give you the desires of your heart. Commit your way to the Lord, trust also in Him, and He shall bring it to pass."

There are things in these verses we must do:

- Trust in the Lord
- Do good
- Dwell in the land
- Feed on His faithfulness
- Delight yourself in the Lord

- Commit your way to the Lord
- Trust in the Lord

As a result of doing these things, God will:

- Give you the desires of your heart
- Bring them to pass

Trust in the Lord (Psalms 37:3 and 5)

Without my even realizing it, God was starting to work in my life to bring about some pretty amazing changes. I was doing many of these things, and the Lord was proving faithful in making things happen. You will notice in this section of verses that our responsibility is wrapped by trusting in the Lord. Trust is a similar concept to faith. Each day we trust something. We trust the chairs we sit in are not going to break. We trust the bank to let us get our money back when our paychecks are deposited into our accounts. In my life, I was trusting God with the outcome of my life by being sure my actions and decisions were based on the instructions from the Bible. Trusting in God means you trust him to take care of you, the way a child trusts its parents to provide food, shelter, and clothing. Children are completely helpless and must rely on their parents for their needs. In many ways, we are much more helpless in this world without God than a baby is without its parents.

Do Good (Psalm 37:3)

According to Isaiah 64:6 our good works are nothing more than filthy rags before the Lord. In order to really do good works, we must first have the Holy Spirit dwelling inside us. Then we have to know what good is. When God created the world, after each step in creation it says in Genesis, "And God saw that it was good." God's creation, all of it, including man, was good before sin came into the world. According to Webster's, good is defined as "complete or sufficiently perfect in its kind, having moral qualities best adapted to its design or use, conformable to moral law, useful, pleasant to the taste, full, complete, honorable, or unblemished." So, in order to do good, as defined by this Scripture, we must first understand what God's unique purpose is for our lives. Generally speaking, every Christian woman is called to obey God; respect her husband; have a chaste and gentle spirit; set an example for her children; display the fruit of the Spirit; and manage the household in a way that honors God and her family. This is a good starting point for learning how to do good.

Dwell in the Land (Psalm 37:3)

So what is it to dwell with the Lord? The Lord is a holy God, and we are not holy. No human has ever been in the presence of the Lord and lived to tell about it. The most amazing story about being in God's presence is in Exodus 19. The Lord tells Moses to purify the people, for He is going to come to Moses at the top of the mountain. The people were not even to touch the base of the mountain as they would die from the holiness of the Lord. Yet Moses was instructed to climb the mountain. "There were thunderings and lightnings, and a thick cloud on the mountain. Now Mount Sinai was completely in smoke, because the Lord descended upon it in fire … and the whole mountain quaked greatly. Then the Lord came down upon Mount Sinai, and the Lord called Moses to the top of the mountain, and Moses went up. Now the glory of the Lord rested on Mount Sinai, and the cloud covered it six days. The sight of the glory of the Lord was like a consuming fire on the top of the mountain in the eyes of the children of Israel. Now it was so, when Moses came down from Mount Sinai that Moses did not know that the skin of his face shone while he talked with Him."— Exodus 24:16, 18; Exodus 34:29

Moses was changed by dwelling with the Lord on top of the mountain. Moses had experienced the glory of God, and when he descended, his face shone with the glory of God. Moses was a mirror of God's glory to the people, and it scared them. Is it possible to dwell with the Lord and not be changed?

There are many examples in Scripture on how the Lord cleans and purifies us. One is directly related to biblical womanhood. Proverbs 31:10 says, "Who can find a virtuous wife? For her worth is far above rubies."

Have you ever wondered how rubies become so beautiful? When rubies are found in the mine, they are ugly and have layers of dirt on them. They are first washed and scrubbed in warm soapy water. Then they are placed under a bright light for inspection, showing all the black stuff that hides the beautiful stones inside. Rubies are covered in a material called matrix, which is the gray/black stuff on the outside. The matrix is removed by chipping it away. Then the rubies are thrown into a rock tumbler to tumble against each other. The stones hit each other and break loose the matrix material. The rubies don't break, as they are harder than the matrix. Then to perfect the stones, they are tumbled again with polishing grit to finalize the process.

So it is with our lives. In order for us to be made holy, in order for us to allow the beautiful parts to shine through, the Lord must scrub us and chip away the sin. As the gem maker, He must reach into our lives and chip away the ugly pieces during our beautification process. This is never a pain-free process but is well worth the results. Then He "tumbles us" against other Christians so that we may be more like Christ each day. What a beautiful picture of Christian fellowship. All Christians have a beautiful, shiny stone inside them just waiting to get out, and we are all covered by ugly sin on the outside, just like the ruby is covered with matrix. The Lord brings us together "to tumble against each other" so the sin is being removed and we all become beautiful in the Lord. This is a lifelong process as we will never be pure while we are living in this fallen world, but no matter where you are in your walk, you will always need fellowship to help you remove the sin from your life. You may be in the beginning stages of your walk or you may be in the later stages, but it does not matter as we can all "tumble against each other" to remove the sin in our life.

Another picture of what happens to us when we dwell with the Lord is that of silver being refined. Psalm 66:10 says, "For You, O God, have tested us; You have refined us as silver is refined." Malachi 3:3 says, "He will sit as a refiner and a purifier of silver."

There was a group of women in a Bible study group discussing the book of Malachi. As they were studying chapter 3, they came across verse 3, which says: "He will sit as a refiner and purifier of silver." This verse puzzled the women, and they wondered what this statement meant about the character and nature of God.

One of the women offered to find out the process of refining silver and get back to the group at their next Bible study. That week, this woman called up a silversmith and made an appointment to watch him at work.

She didn't mention anything about the reason for her interest beyond her curiosity about the process of refining silver. As she watched the silversmith, he held a piece of silver over the fire and let it heat up. He explained that in refining silver, one needed to hold the silver in the middle of the fire where the flames were hottest as to burn away all the impurities. The woman thought about God holding us in such a hot spot, and then she thought again about the verse, "He sits as a refiner and purifier of silver." She asked the silversmith if it was true that he had to sit in front of the fire the whole time the silver was being refined. The man answered that yes, he not only had to sit there holding the silver, he had to keep his eyes on the silver the entire time it was in the fire. If the silver was left a moment too long in the flames, it would be destroyed. The woman was silent for a moment. Then she asked the silversmith, "How do you know when the silver is fully refined?" He smiled at her and answered, "Oh, that's easy—when I see my image in it."

If today you are feeling the heat of the fire, remember that God has His eye on you and will keep watching you until He sees His image in you. (Excerpt from http://www.christianguitar.org/forums/t12075/, accessed July 2010) [13]

All of these analogies on dwelling with God drive home the point that the image of God shines through us. When Moses came down from the mountain, Moses was shining due to the holiness of God. When rubies are cleaned, they allow the beauty within to shine through. The beauty within us is the Holy Spirit. When silver is purified, the silversmith is able to see his image in it. So dwelling with God may cause much discomfort in this sinful world, but it will produce eternal results.

Feed on His Faithfulness (Psalm 37:3)

We are to feed on God's faithfulness. The most obvious example of feeding on something is the process of eating. When we eat something, many things must happen for that to be successful. First we must pick that something up and bring it to our mouths. Then we must take a bite, chew it, and swallow it. Then our body takes over and absorbs all the nutrients.

The same is true when we feed on God's faithfulness. We must pick up and open our Bibles. We read what God's word says, and our minds must absorb what God's word is saying to us. God's faithfulness is eternal, not temporary like the faithfulness I had experienced. God's faithfulness is something I could rely on when I could rely on nothing else in this world, because God exists outside this world and chooses to put His presence in our world through the Holy Spirit. God's faithfulness provides nourishment for the soul that nothing on Earth can provide.

Delight Yourself in the Lord (Psalm 37:4)

Have you ever delighted yourself in the Lord? There is a story in Psalms where David was said to be running down the street naked, praising God. I think we would be arrested today and sent to a mental institution if we were to do that. But there is something to be said about enjoying the presence of the Lord.

Have you ever had a perfect day? A beautiful day where maybe you went to the beach or to a historic site? The weather was perfect. You did not think about yesterday and you did not think about tomorrow. You just enjoyed what you were doing in the moment. What about when you have quiet time or read a good book? This is what God wants us to do when we read the Bible. He wants us to sit and enjoy the moment with Him. He delights in us each time we spend time with Him. It is a two-way relationship, and He is always there for us. Yet we also have to be there for Him. I have to believe it brings the Lord much pleasure when we just sit and delight in His presence. He wants to bring us the peace and joy that comes from delighting in Him and not worrying about yesterday or tomorrow.

I spent two weeks on a mission trip in Egypt where nothing mattered except for what I was doing each second. I did not worry about tomorrow, just who I was talking to each moment. My conversations with individuals who did not know Jesus could have affected eternity, and being on the foreign mission field took away all pressures of daily life. This is part of delighting in Christ—just making sure each second brings honor and glory to Him and letting Him work out the details in life.

Commit Your Way to the Lord (Psalm 37:5)

The last part of the verse tells us to commit your way to the Lord. This is where the Lord took my personality trait of being stubborn and used it for a good thing. Usually, people who are stubborn use it for something negative. Stubbornness is associated with donkeys that want to get their own way. I spent many years trying to get my own way, and it did not lead down a good road. But the Lord took this negative personality trait and used it to give me strength to be committed to Him. I became fully committed to the way of the Lord. The Lord's way became my way. The Lord's way was for me to stay married, to love someone who did not love me, and to learn from the experience. No one around me really understood it, but they seemed to respect me for it. As everyone found out later in life, I made a drastic change in my life that would have never been so huge had I not learned how to commit my way to the Lord.

During the first couple of years of my turmoil, one of my heart's deep desires was for my husband to experience a relationship with the Lord the way I had. Later I just wanted him to go away. Then I just wanted to do God's will. I knew he was miserable because he was seeking fulfillment that I and the world could not give him. I gave up my personal happiness so my husband could be exposed to the gospel.

"For I know that this will turn out for my deliverance through your prayer and the supply of the Spirit of Jesus Christ, according to my earnest expectation and hope that in nothing I shall be ashamed, but with all boldness, as always, so now also Christ will be magnified in my body, whether by life or by death. For to me, to live is Christ, and to die is gain. But if I live on in the flesh, this will mean fruit from my labor; yet what I shall choose I cannot tell. For I am hard-pressed between the two, having a desire to depart and be with Christ, which is far better. Nevertheless to remain in the flesh is more needful for you."—Philippians 1:19–24

I had an acute awareness that I was the only Christian my husband knew. He knew my imperfections. He could see Christ working in my life. What Philippians showed me was that my body was Christ's. It was no longer I who lived in me, but the Holy Spirit. The Holy Spirit had to work through me in order for my husband to get exposure to the gospel. If Christ was crucified and died for me, why should the expectation be any different for me? What was more important, my personal comfort or obedience to God? We live in a society where personal comfort comes quickly. If you are hot, turn on the air conditioner. If you have a headache, take some medicine. However, Christ suffered greatly for our salvation. Why should I have expected no suffering if I was to make an impact on the world for Christ? I was committed to God, and I was committed to allow God to work through me. I gave up much personal comfort so that one person, who should have been the most important person in my life, could have exposure to the gospel.

Desires of Your Heart (Psalm 37:4)

Now we get to see what the Lord will do. While the Lord's list is much shorter, it is actually much more difficult. The Lord will give us the desires of our heart and will bring them to pass. What an awesome statement! If He gives us a desire, He is going to make it happen. All we have to do is let it happen.

Tithing

First, let's talk about my desire to tithe. If you remember, I am deeply in debt. My monthly payments exceed my income each month. I don't pay more than interest on most of my debt. I had $30,000 in unsecured debt, a husband who rarely worked, and a house payment. It was pretty ridiculous to think that I could give 10 percent of my gross income to the church. I did the math and this was 15 percent of my take home pay. So I did the only thing I knew how to do. I started praying. I prayed Lord, I want to tithe, but I can't. Then, the Lord not only gave me the desire to tithe, he pointed out I was sinning if I did not tithe.

"'Will a man rob God? Yet you have robbed Me! But you say, In what way have we robbed You? In tithes and offerings. You are cursed with a curse, for you have robbed Me, even this whole nation. Bring all the tithes into the storehouse, that there may be food in My house, and try Me now in this,' says the Lord of hosts, 'if I will not open for you the windows of heaven and pour out for you such blessing that there will not be room enough to receive it.'"—Malachi 3:8–10

So now I had a desire to tithe and to not rob God. My pastor taught this Scripture and pointed out that this is the only place in the Bible where God says to test Him. He challenged us that if we were not tithing, we should test God. I still did not have the faith to jump off the cliff of tithing and give 15% of my take home pay to the church. I kept praying and praying and praying. I did not have the strength to let go of the little income I had. The Lord kept laying a burden on my heart. Slowly, I started giving a little to the church. I started with twenty-five dollars twice a month. While I earned more than that, I wanted to give more. Each time I gave the twenty-five dollars, I was still able to pay my bills, even though the numbers did not add up. I eventually worked my way up to fifty dollars twice a month. I was still able to pay my bills. This is where my tithing settled down for a while.

During this time of learning to tithe, my husband moved out of the house again. It was a time period of about eighteen months. I had to walk the fine line between obeying God and being submissive to my husband. If you examine the priorities of God being your first love, and then your husband, you must first and foremost obey God's commands. God commands us to tithe. He also commands us to be submissive to our husbands. So I decided to obey God and try to tithe.

At the same time I'm learning to tithe, the church advertised a trip to Egypt. As soon as the announcement was made from the pulpit, I knew deep down in my heart I would be going. I continually felt so drawn to the trip and felt such compassion toward the women of Egypt who did not appear to have loving relationships with their husband. My most vivid memory in the decision making process was a Time article called 'The Women of Islam' that laid out marriage examples for Iran and Pakistan. I so wanted to provide some encouragement, yet I knew I could never afford the $1,800 that was required to go. So I started praying. I know you are not supposed to make deals with God, but I did not know what else to do. I prayed, "Lord, if you help me go to Egypt without my taking on any more debt, I will start tithing."

During the next few months, several things happened. First, I got a $1,000 bonus at work. After taxes, I was able to put $750 toward my mission trip. The funny thing was, this bonus did not even come out of my department's budget. It came from an outside source. I worked for government at the time, and bonuses were not a regular occurrence. Then we did several fundraisers and sent out donation request letters. I ended up raising $2,100 and was able to help pay for someone else to go on the trip with the extra funds.

I knew it was time to take the leap off the cliff of faith and start tithing. So I started giving 10 percent of my gross pay, even though I was sure I could not afford it. The amazing thing was, I could still pay my bills even with about 15 percent less of my net income. I discovered that tithing is an act of faith and obedience. It is not something you can necessarily afford; however, if you don't do it, you can't start the abundant life Jesus says He came to give us.

My financial situation continued to dramatically improve after I started tithing. I tested God, and He poured out his blessing. Even after years, the numbers in my financial situation never add up, but I always tithe, and somehow, I'm always able to pay my bills.

Submission

My next desire was to submit to a godly husband. This desire became one of the deepest of my heart. I studied the concept of submission in great detail and tried to live it out with my unbelieving husband. The challenge in my situation was that he was not willing to exert any leadership. He knew he did not want to be married to me for the rest of his life, so he would not make any decisions that had more than one day's consequence. If he made a decision exerting any leadership, it was always a selfish motive, such as wanting to buy a vehicle or transmission or some other thing that would put us further in debt.

I explained the concepts of submission and leadership to him and tried to encourage him with positive words every way I could. I knew I could not nag him into exerting leadership. Every time a decision had to be made, I would ask him what he thought. If he was knowledgable about a particular type of purchase, I would ask him to make the decision and compliment him to try to give him confidence. If I could find any positive characteristic in him, I would compliment that characteristic and build it up.

However, Psalm 127:1 says that unless the Lord builds the house, the laborers labor in vain. It definitely seemed that the Lord was not building my house with this man as I continued to labor in vain. However, I was determined to be a godly wife. If I could not be a godly wife in the circumstance the Lord had placed me in, I would not be a godly wife in any situation. The Lord had to first trust me with a small task before He would trust me with something bigger.

There is a saying that the man is the head of the home and the woman is the heart. I've heard it many times in church presentations and conferences from the godliest of wives. Every time I heard that expression, it was said by a person married to a believer.

In Stormie Omartian's book *The Power of a Praying Wife*, she devotes a couple of pages to this topic. The first chapter is devoted to the wife, and how we need to change before God can change our husband. It is actually the longest chapter in the book. She writes that a wife's responsibility as the heart of the home is to make it a peaceful sanctuary—a source of contentment, acceptance, rejuvenation, nurturing, rest, and love for your entire family. A sanctuary is a place of protection and an escape from the world we can go to each day. I worked very hard to create this environment for my husband and allowed God to be the head of my home until God gave me a husband who could be the head of my home.

As I tried to live out this principle while being married to an unbeliever, I learned some difficult lessons while trying to be the heart of the home. In peeling back one more layer to this expression, I came to the conclusion that while we have earthly roles to fulfill based on Scripture, we need God to actually be the heart and the head of the home. Without God's help, I was completely powerless to be the heart of the home. I desperately needed to spend time with God each and every day to bring the fruit of the Spirit into my home. The fruits of the Spirit were the only thing that allowed me to create any type of sanctuary for my husband. On several occasions, my husband would leave me because I successfully created this sanctuary for him, and he said he felt he did not deserve it. In the midst of all the pain, God was teaching me to be a godly wife regardless of how my husband acted.

Ephesians outlines the fruit we produce from God's spirit. "But the fruit of the Spirit is love, joy, peace, longsuffering, kindness, goodness, faithfulness, gentleness, self-control. Against such, there is no law. And those who are Christ's have crucified the flesh with its passions and desires."—Ephesians 6:22–24

During this phase of my life, I was privileged with the opportunity to teach a Bible lesson on the fruit of the Spirit. We looked at the definition of each of the fruits listed and talked about how they impacted our lives.

The first fruit of the Spirit is love. One Corinthians 13 offers the most beautiful explanation of love: love is patient, kind, does not envy, does not boast, is not proud, is not rude, is not self-seeking, is not easily angered, keeps no record of wrongs, does not delight in evil, always protects, always trusts, always hopes, always perseveres. The Spirit of God can only produce love in us. It is not a feeling or an emotion or anything that meets our needs. It is an outward action to put others first. One little word, yet so much meaning that we don't understand in our culture today.

Love (Webster's 1828 Dictionary)	
Patient	Having the quality of enduring evils without murmuring or fretfulness; not easily provoked, not hasty.
Kind	Disposed to do good to others; supplying their wants or assisting them in distress; proceeding from tenderness or goodness of the heart.
Does not Envy	Does not feel uneasiness or discontent at the sight of superior excellence, reputation, or happiness enjoyed by another; does not fret or grieve one's self at the real or supposed superiority of another.
Is not Proud	Does not have inordinate self-esteem; does not possess a high or unreasonable conceit of one's own excellence.
Is not Rude	Is not rough, is not of course manners or unpolished.
Is not Self-Seeking	Does not seek one's own interest or happiness.
Keeps no Record of Wrongs	This concept relates to "forgive and forget." Love not only forgives, it forgets the offense and works toward reconciliation Hebrews 8:12 says "For I will forgive their wickedness and will remember their sins no more" (NIV).

Does not Delight in Evil	Does not delight in having bad qualities of a moral kind, not wicked, not corrupt, not perverse.
Rejoices in truth	To gladden or delight in conformity to fact or reality. Jesus Christ was called the truth.
Always Protects	Always covers or shields from danger or injury.
Always Trusts	Always has confidence; reliance or resting of the mind on the integrity, veracity, justice, friendship, or other sound principle of another person.
Always Hopes	Always has a desire of some good or confidence in a future event due to God's working in your life.
Always Perseveres	Always continues in a state of grace.

Have you every met anyone who displays even half these characteristics all the time or even part of the time? Wouldn't you want to always be around that kind of person? Can you imagine putting all of these characteristics into one person who is also all-powerful, all-knowing, and all-present? According to 1 Corinthians 13, God *is* love. This means He knows and is able to meet our needs before we know what they are. He meets so many of our needs that we don't even think about. Our hearts keep pumping blood, our bodies know how to breathe, and the oceans stay within their borders. He kindly meets our needs that we are not even conscious of having. God is not proud. Have you ever met a humble person who is also all-powerful? That combination doesn't exist on Earth. Has someone always protected you every second from getting hurt? I can't even imagine being in such an awesome presence. Yet as you seek God, you will get to be in the fullness of His presence one day. He is our true "knight in shining armor" that we dreamed of as little girls.

No wonder the Bible says there will be no more death or mourning or crying or pain in heaven. We will be in a place without sin. We will be in a place without disappointment. While I still can't imagine how awesome that will be, I am glad to know that my deceased loved ones are in a place that is full of hope and joy and that they are always protected.

Husbands are commanded to love their wives, and wives are called to respect their husbands. It would be so easy to love and respect a husband who lived this way. Yet as hard as any husband tries, he is not God. That is why we must lift him up in prayer, and look to God to meet our needs. It puts too much of a burden on our husbands if we expect them to meet the needs of our inner being that only God can meet. This is why God is truly the head and heart of the home. Whether our husbands are believers or unbelievers, only God can truly love us the way it is described in Scripture.

The other fruits of the Spirit are joy, peace, longsuffering, kindness, goodness, faithfulness, gentleness, and self-control. All of the following definitions are taken from Webster's 1828 American Dictionary.

Fruits of the Spirit	
Joy	The passion or emotion excited by the expectation of good; the gratification of desire.
Peace	A state of quiet or tranquility; freedom from disturbance or agitation.
Longsuffering	Bearing injuries or provocation for a long time; not easily provoked.
Kindness	That temper or disposition which delights in contributing to the happiness of others.
Goodness	The moral qualities, which constitute Christian excellence; moral virtue.
Faithfulness	Fidelity; loyalty; firm adherence to allegiance and duty; truth; veracity; as the faithfulness of God.
Gentleness	Softness of manners; mildness of temper; sweetness of disposition.
Self-Control	Not in the dictionary. However, "control" is power, authority, and command. We are to control our power, authority, and command of others.

As I read through the list of the fruits produced by the Spirit, I became convinced that the Lord needed to do a great work in me. Oh, how I want these characteristics to be part of who I am! I never consistently displayed the fruit of the Spirit in my life. I felt like a very ugly person. So I put these definitions on my refrigerator, read them each day, and asked the Lord to change me. I wanted to become a person who displayed the Spirit to the world. I don't know if I was in the best place or the worst place to learn how to do these things, but the Lord knew I was in the perfect place. When I showed love and it was not returned, I had to bear the injury of my feelings being hurt. I constantly reached out to my husband and tried to create a sanctuary for him. And he constantly built relationships with everyone he could outside the home. If he was at home, he was in the back yard working on his vehicles. If he happened to be in the house when he got a phone call, he would go outside to take the call. It was not a healthy relationship.

My realization was that I could control myself. I could not control the circumstances I was in. I was envious of those women I knew who had good marriages—even the ones where both were living the lives of unbelievers. At least their husband was their friend.

Prior to listing the fruits of the Spirit, Paul listed the fruit of the flesh in Ephesians 6. They included items such as adultery, fornication, uncleanness, lewdness, idolatry, sorcery, hatred, contentions, jealousies, outbursts of wrath, selfish ambitions, dissensions, heresies, envy, murders, drunkenness, revelries, and the like. In my household, my husband frequently produced fruit of the flesh. He was a difficult person to live with on a daily basis. At times, I'm sure I was not an easy person to live with either, but I was praying for the Lord to do a good work through me.

I would have much preferred to live in the household of individuals who were producing fruit of the Spirit and not fruit of the flesh. The Lord convicted me of how important it was that His Spirit be the heart of the home. Likewise, it was also His Spirit that had to be the head of the home. I obeyed God and enlisted the principles taught in Scripture to the best of my ability.

The following Scriptures talk about God's design for marriage: "Wives, submit to your own husbands, as to the Lord. For the husband is head of the wife, as also Christ is head of the church; and He is the Savior of the body. Therefore, just as the church is subject to Christ, so let the wives be to their own husbands in everything. Husbands, love your wives, just as Christ also loved the church and gave Himself for her, that he might sanctify and cleanse her with the washing of water by the word, that he might present her to Himself a glorious church, not having spot or wrinkle or any such thing, but that she should be holy and without blemish. So husbands ought to love their own wives as their own bodies; he who loves his wife loves himself. For no one ever hated his own flesh, but nourishes and cherishes it, just as the Lord does the church. For we are members of His body, of His flesh and of His bones. For this reason a man shall leave his father and mother and be joined to his wife, and the two shall become one flesh. This is a great mystery, but I speak concerning Christ and the church. Nevertheless let each one of you in particular so love his own wife as himself, and let the wife see that she respect her husband."—Ephesians 6:22–33

This passage of Scripture, as well as a couple others we will review, are probably the best "marriage manuals" out there. Do you know why? Because God designed us and knows us better than we know ourselves. He made us this way and is telling us how things work best.

First, we'll talk about the wives' responsibility. The last line probably sums up the husband's biggest need from his wife: respect. He needs to know that out of all the people in the world, his wife respects him. She may share her opinions on decisions and may not agree with all he does, but in the end, his decision stands, and she carries it out wholeheartedly. He needs to have his wife trust in his every move. Nowhere does it command the wife to love her husband, just respect him. That is because as women, it is naturally easy to love our husbands. It is not as easy to respect them. Every day I would wonder if I would come home and see my husband packing to move out again. The only love I could show him was Christ's love. But I was still his wife and made every effort to fulfill my responsibilities as a wife. By doing so I was obeying God. I decided that if I could not be a good wife to an ungodly husband, I would also not be a good wife to a godly husband. I settled in for the long haul until God led me elsewhere.

The book of Genesis sheds some light on why it is so difficult for us to respect our husbands. In Genesis, Adam and Eve were thrown out of the Garden of Eden. God cursed women with the following: "To the women He said, I will greatly multiply your sorrow and your conception; in pain you shall bring forth children; Your desire shall be for your husband, And he shall rule over you."—Genesis 3:16

When it says your desire shall be for your husband, that translates into "our desire will be to rule over our husbands." The Lord cursed women into wanting to do things our way! He cursed us into making it difficult for us to respect our husbands. He cursed us into having a daily struggle making us, and our husbands, miserable. The sooner we realize this and try to submit to our husbands and to God, the sooner we will experience less of the curse. We will find some freedom from this sin that keeps us bound in chains. Not that it will ever go away, but loose chains are a lot easier to live with than the tight chains that are cutting into our skin.

The passage of Scripture in Ephesians gave wives one thing to do in different words: submit and respect their husbands. When we submit to and respect our husbands, we submit to and respect God. Submission and respect in this passage are one and the same. The command for husbands is to love their wives as Christ loved the church. This command has several implications in this passage of Scripture.

First, it gives husbands the responsibility to be the head of the home and the teacher of their wives. It tells husbands to love their wives the way Christ loves the church. This is a much harder command to follow then the one given to wives. It literally says that the husband must be willing to be tortured and die for their wives.

When Christ lived on this earth, He did several things for the church. He taught the church by explaining Scripture. Our husbands have the responsibility to teach us. Christ always pointed back to the Father, and our husbands have the responsibility to point us back to God. Christ humbled himself, became a baby, lived a poor life, showed us the meaning of service by washing his disciples' feet, and died on the cross. Christ put the needs of the church above his own needs each day. This is what a Christian husband is called to do for his wife. This is an immensely difficult task. Imagine how much easier our husband's jobs are if we encourage him to live up to this role and joyfully submit to what he is trying to do.

This Scripture teaches us that we are all one body in the church. In the same way, husbands and wives are one flesh. If we tear our husbands down, we are tearing ourselves down. If we do not respect our husbands, we are not respecting ourselves. If our husbands do not love us, they also do not love themselves. It is amazing to think that when spouses hurt each other, they are also hurting themselves.

"A quarrelsome wife is like a constant dripping on a rainy day."—Proverbs 27:15

"Enjoy life with the woman whom you love all the days of your fleeting life which He has given to you under the sun; for this is your reward in life and in your toil in which you have labored under the sun."—Ecclesiastes 9:9 (New American Standard)

Have you ever had something get on your last nerve and just would not stop? Maybe it was a neighbor's dog barking in the middle of the night when you have to get up, or someone else's music waking your baby. Proverbs say that a quarrelsome wife is like a constant dripping that will not go away. Then, Ecclesiastes says that as wives, we are our husbands' gift from God. When I read this Scripture the first time, I was overwhelmed with humility that I would be my husband's gift from God. I had this deep desire to be a good gift and not a constant dripping. It is so convicting to think that every word we say, every good or bad thing we do for our husbands is from a gift he received. Do you want to be the gift that is cherished or the one your husband wishes he never received?

"You husbands in the same way, live with your wives in an understanding way, as with someone weaker, since she is a woman; and show her honor as a fellow heir of the grace of life, so that your prayers will not be hindered."—I Peter 3:7

For me, it is humbling to think that my husband's prayers could be hindered because of me. Nowhere in Scripture does it say that a wife's prayers will be hindered based on how she treats her husband. Here it tells our husbands how to treat us so that their prayers will not be hindered! If you are married to a believer, that should give you great encouragement to respect him, encourage him, and give him every opportunity for his prayers not to be hindered. As the head of the home, he is responsible for our children and us. I can only imagine how much a truly godly man worries about the spiritual well-being of his family. It is our job to make that load as light as possible.

At this point, if you are married to an unbeliever, you may be wondering how God could be the head of the home when your husband is not a believer. Scripture does not say to submit to your husband if he is a believer. You must do your best to submit to your husband, because in so doing, you are submitting to and obeying God. Disobedience to God will not improve your situation, as you are then living outside the will of God. The safest place to live is in the will of God.

So what do you do when your husband makes a decision you do not agree with? What do you do when your husband is not a believer? You respect him and pray. I can't tell you how many times I had to respect a decision my unbelieving husband made that I did not agree with. Occasionally, he would get a job for a few weeks and would make the decision to take his entire paycheck and buy something to resell so he could make the money go further. Over and over again, we would be stuck with whatever he bought, which usually resulted in a non-functioning car, truck, or boat being parked in the yard. I would be reminded of these poor decisions for years. But I had to trust God to be my provider and trust God to protect me when I was submitting to my husband. I would express my disagreement, then pray about it and move forward with whatever decision he made. Many times he would come to me a day or so later and say, "I changed my mind."

The Lord protected me from many of the worst decisions. God proved Himself to me over and over as the head of my home. I would be agonizing inside over a course of action and begging and praying to God. So many times I would be saying, "Lord, you have commanded me to respect my husband, but I do not agree with this decision." Before having a chance to take any action or get tired of waiting and open my mouth, my husband would alter his course of action. Sometimes it would take every ounce of self-control I had to not take action to fix the situation. The harder it was for me to not take action, the more God proved Himself to me by fixing the situation. This is when I came to the realization that God is the head of the home whether you are married to a believer or an unbeliever. God looked out for me so many times when I obeyed His word by respecting my husband.

There is a point where you have to trust that God is sovereign and in control. We all like to think we control our own lives. We hold on as tight as we can and try to control the outcome of every situation. Once we realize life is so much easier when we just let go and let God be in control, we start to feel the burden of the world lift from our shoulders.

One way to let go is to hold your hands up in the air like you are lifting all your cares in life and giving them to God. Hold your hands as tight as you can, like you are not letting go. Now pray, "God, I know I cannot control my life, but you can. So I am letting go of these worries and giving them to you." Now release the grip of your hands and wait to feel the relief. I promise it will come if you are sincere in your prayer. You may have to do this prayer many times a day until it becomes a habit not to hold on to your worries so tightly, but once you finally let go and let God, you will start to enjoy the freedom of resting in the arms of our Savior.

The things that you do have control over are your own actions, decisions, attitudes, and willingness to obey God. You have the choice to obey or disobey God. God will not force Himself on you. But since you are reading this book, I can guarantee you God wants to perform miracles in your life like the ones He has done in mine.

Chapter 6

Contentment

As I continued growing in the fruit of the Spirit each day and learned just how much God loved me, the whirlwind of life around me grew stronger each day. Each evening I would sit on my couch with my 110-gallon fish aquarium across from me. I would listen to a couple of "praise songs" with my dog sitting at my feet and watch my fish swimming around. I could appreciate the wonder of God's creation in this atmosphere. I would light a candle to mask my husband's cigarette smoke smell in the house. Then I would just relax. I had my devotional book and journal next to me. I would ask God to speak to me and would read the devotional and hope I had something to write.

I kept my eyes on the things of heaven but struggled daily with the direction my life was going in. Was this how things would be for the rest of my life? Would I spend the next sixty years married to someone who did not love me? I felt I was fighting a huge invisible battle I could not escape. I so desperately wanted some direction to my life. When I prayed and meditated on the future, I did not feel God's call to spend my whole life in this situation, yet God did not release me, either. God, in my heart, kept telling me I had to obey Him no matter what.

"For I know that this will turn out for my deliverance through your prayer and the supply of the Spirit of Jesus Christ, according to my earnest expectation and hope that in nothing I shall be ashamed, but with all boldness, as always, so now also Christ will be magnified in my body, whether by life or by death. For to me, to live is Christ and to die is gain. But if I live on in the flesh, this will mean fruit from my labor; yet what I shall choose I cannot tell. For I am hard-pressed between the two, having a desire to depart and be with Christ, which is far better."—Philippians 1:19-24

As I prayed, the message never really changed. God kept telling me it was His Spirit living in me. My physical discomfort on this Earth would be limited. I wanted my circumstance to change, but God said wait. I was so dissatisfied with my marriage, the constant tearing each other apart, the constant burden of being married to someone that hated God that I truly felt to die would be gain as I had already died to any desire of anything on this earth. Most individuals have a future planned for themselves which ties them to this earth. I had no future planned for myself as I just lived from day to day trying to express the love of God. My only future that I looked forward to was the one in Heaven with no pain, no sin, and no sadness. I felt so weak in the flesh. My job was to pray for my husband and trust God. It was so hard to wait for God's outcome day in and day out.

There is an illusion in this world that a content person has everything he or she wants. A content person has his or her desired marriage, desired job, desired house, and desired car. However, I found that contentment was quite a different concept. The lies of the enemy had invaded me, and invaded most of those who live in our world.

In order to understand my long journey to contentment, I had to first understand my source of discontent. What desires in life did I have that were not being fulfilled? Where was I not satisfied in the Lord? Where was my faith wavering where the Lord had placed me? Why did I want more when I should be content in having an awesome relationship with the Lord? What is the peace that surpasses all understanding, and where does it come from?

As I prayed, I learned that my first source of discontentment was that I did not really trust God. While I had a huge measure of faith and mentally knew that God had the power to do anything, I did not believe He *would* do anything. I did not trust in my heart of hearts that God would take care of me. I still liked to give God advice. I thought I knew better than

God what direction my life needed to go and when it needed to go there. I did not completely trust His plan. This takes us back to Psalm 37:4, "He shall give you the desires of your heart, and He shall bring it to pass." My struggle was that I knew what my heart's desires were, but I did not trust God's timing in bringing them to pass. I wanted so much to be married to a godly man, who loved and cherished me and wanted to raise a godly family together. I wanted it right now. My desire was also to obey God no matter what the cost. At this particular point in time, those two desires seemed to be in direct conflict and impossible. It seemed I could not have the desires of my heart without disobeying God. Above all, God wants our loyalty and obedience (Hosea 6:6). So, I had to learn to be content.

When we walk with the Lord, it is like walking on a stone walkway. However, we only get enough direction toward the next stone. And until we step on that next stone, the view does not change. We don't get to see what is on the second or third stone. God gets to see the whole path and where it is going, and we only get to see the next step. We have to take a leap of faith and actually take the step God is showing us without knowing where the path goes after that. Until we take the first step, we are blind as to any further progress down the path. The longer it takes for us to take that step, the longer and slower our progress is in moving down the path of life.

I spent years not taking the steps the Lord was showing me. I would take a step to the right or to the left, but not the one the Lord wanted me to take. As a result, the next step the Lord placed in front of me for my Christian walk always stayed the same until I actually took that step.

As a senior in high school, the Lord sent a friend into my life who tried to convince me I was not dating a good person. I was fifteen years old. My friend approached me in the hallway at school and said, "I don't want to lose your friendship, but your boyfriend tried to make a move on me." I was sure she misunderstood something he said. When I approached him about it, he convinced me she did misunderstand, and I lost my friend.

Five years later, I had a very good friend who was a co-worker. When our friendship started, I was not married and had no boyfriend. My ex-boyfriend was living about two hours away, and it seemed life was on the right track. However, my ex-boyfriend moved back to town to be with me. We all tried to be friends, but the two of them did not get along. She was honest with me about his character, and he convinced me that she was the one who had a bad character. Again, I lost another friendship.

So the Lord gave me two opportunities to take the step I needed to take. It was the exact same step both times. I needed to let go of the person I was dating. The Lord wanted me to be in love with Him, not anything on this earth. Yet I did not know what that meant and did not trust myself as a single woman. I stepped to the right and to the left and ended up in a terrible marriage. It took several years of brokenness before I could learn to blindly take the steps the Lord wanted me to take. Then, once I finally learned to take the steps the Lord wanted me to take, I could run down the path instead of crawling or going in the wrong direction. The Lord's leading became clearer and clearer. My sensitivity to the Holy Spirit became clear to me. It was a gift the Lord gave me through many years of brokenness.

"And the Lord, He is the One who goes before you. He will be with you, He will not leave you nor forsake you; do not fear nor be dismayed."—Deuteronomy 31:8

At the same time I was learning to walk the path of life with God, I also started having more desires that did not follow the direction of life my husband wanted to go. I had turned thirty and now desired to have children. The biological clock I never had before started ticking! I was an only child and an only grandchild. I had no one to take care of me when I got older. When my parents passed away, I would have no family from either side. I would be alone in this world when I got older.

It all started with my grandmother's death. I had been married about two years. At Christmas, we went to visit Granny, who was living at home with a nurse to help take care of her. She was too weak to get out of bed, so Mom and I went to sit beside her bedside. We had watched her grow weaker and weaker over the last couple of years.

About a week after Christmas, the nurse pulled Mom aside and said she saw symptoms that we should probably take her to the hospital and she would not be coming out. The first day in the hospital, she could acknowledge my presence. The second day, she could not. I sat and talked to her and told her I loved her. I told her if she needed to go home to heaven, it was okay.

I could not visit her the third day due to the emotions. I begged my husband to go with me. He would not go. He said, "You know I don't like hospitals." I drove alone on the fourth day to the hospital. By this time I was physically and emotionally exhausted. I visited with her about a half an hour, held her hand, and gave her a kiss on the cheek before I left. I whispered in her ear that I loved her and that it was okay to go. The hallway in the hospital seemed a mile long. I walked out to the car almost in tears. I finally made it to the parking lot and sat down in the driver's seat of my car. I just broke down crying. I knew I would miss her terribly. She died a day and a half later.

As a result of my granny's death, I started having a desire to have two children by the time I was thirty-five. This vision was unusual considering I never previously wanted to have children.

I talked to my husband about this, and he said no way. He said, "I can't take care of myself, do you expect to take care of a child?"

He was right. I did not want to be a single mom, and I did not want my children growing up with a dad who treated them the way I was treated. I thought it would be cruel to bring children into a world where they would receive this look each day that their dad wished they never existed. I tried to find other things to occupy my thoughts. This desire never left my heart, but I had to let it go. I asked my friend Katrina to pray for me, and since she was battling with infertility, she was compassionate in a way that no one else could have been at that point in my life. The Lord had provided the perfect friend for this situation. We lived close enough that we could meet and walk together for about forty-five minutes in the evening. We would talk about the desire for children, God's plan for marriage, and politics as it affected a Christian worldview. She especially understood the desire to have children since she and her husband had been trying for years to become pregnant.

This desire was causing great discontentment with my situation. I realized that if the Lord wanted me to be alone in my old age, I would be alone in my old age.

I read 1 Samuel chapter 1. In this Scripture, a woman named Hannah cannot have children. She was brought to tears over the situation. Out of desperation, she wept in anguish to the Lord. She was so upset, the priest accused her of being drunk in the temple. In verse 11, she says, "O Lord of hosts, if You will indeed look on the affliction of Your maidservant and remember me, and not forget Your maidservant, but will give Your maidservant a male child, then I will give him to the Lord all the days of his life." Hannah gave the Lord her unborn child. Again, I did not trust the path the Lord had for me in life. The Lord kept whispering in my ear that He could take care of me better than children if it was His plan for me not to have children.

"Therefore, I say to you, do not worry about your life, what you will eat, or what you will drink; nor about your body, what you will put on. Is not life more than food and the body more than clothing? Look at the birds of the air, for they neither sow nor reap nor gather into barns; yet your heavenly Father feeds them. Are you not of more value than they? Which of you by worrying can add one cubit to his stature? So why do you worry about clothing? Consider the lilies of the field, how they grow; they neither toil nor spin; and yet I say to you that even Solomon in all his glory was not arrayed like one of these. Now if God so clothes the grass of the field, which today is, and tomorrow is thrown into the oven, will He not much more clothe you, O ye of little faith? Therefore, do not worry, saying, 'What shall we eat?' or 'what shall we drink?' or 'What shall we wear?' For after all these things the Gentiles seek. For your heavenly Father knows that you need all these things. But seek first the kingdom of God and His righteousness, and all these things shall be added to you. Therefore, do not worry about tomorrow, for tomorrow will worry about its own things. Today has enough trouble of its own."—Matthew 6:25–34

The sentence in this Scripture that pierced me to the core was where Christ said, "Ye of little faith." I knew He was talking to me. It was at this point in my life that I lifted up my hands to God and said, "Here, you can have my children that you have not yet given me and may never give to me." I let this desire go and turned it over to God. Each time I had to take a step of faith and trust God's plan, it became a little easier to take the next step. This step on the path was to prove to God that I trusted Him with my future even if I did not know what it was. It also released my desires into His hand to do with as He saw fit. Again, I felt a sense of freedom that I had not previously experienced in this world. Each time I took a step of faith, I started to enjoy more freedom to rest in the Lord and it was a wonderful experience.

It was during this time that my husband moved out of the house again to live in a room at a garage where he was working part-time. I come home from work to him once again packing his things to move out. It seemed every time he took a step forward in life at being a provider for the family, he would give up. Every time he got a job and we started to make some financial progress, he took it as an opportunity to get some space from me.

So he moved into this room at a garage. I never saw the place, but I enjoyed the peace and quiet of my home and being able to have quiet time without having to stop in the middle and change locations if he walked in the door.

Before moving out, my husband decided to do something about the oak trees so I didn't have to rake so many leaves. He cut down about ten trees and stacked the branches in the yard. Over the next few months it was a great gathering place for snakes and mice. In addition, my neighbor left dog food out where the mice could eat it, and they grew to the size of squirrels. They ate through the metal vents in the foundation of my house and started nesting under the house. I had to call in the exterminator, but my dog did a better job at catching the mice than the exterminator, because the mice were too big for the traps set out. The exterminator was impressed with the dog's two kills between his visits.

My back yard was filled with several broken-down vehicles that he had said he was going to use parts for to make into one vehicle. Now they just sat in my yard. I did not have the financial means to clean anything up, and since they weren't my vehicles, I could not really dispose of them. It was quite the mix. While I worked hard on flowerbeds and vegetable gardens to make the home fit my personality, I had this junkyard flare that I had to live with each day. As a little girl, I never envisioned my yard being quite so junky. My dad had always kept our yard neat and tidy while I was growing up, and I had envisioned my adult life being quite similar.

Even with all the clutter I could not clean up, I enjoyed the thought that maybe this time he would be gone for good. Maybe my life would have a new direction. If God made him a Christian husband who would love me, I would have also basked in that miracle. My hope would occasionally flounder at the lack of direction, and then I would regain my focus. I kept trying to make some sort of sense out of my situation by studying the Scripture. The Lord started to show me how His presence would be causing strife in the world.

"Do not think that I came to bring peace on the earth; I did not come to bring peace, but a sword.—Matthew 10:34 (Jesus is speaking)

"So Jesus answered and said, Assuredly I say to you, there is no one who has left house or brothers or sisters or father or mother or wife or children or lands, for My sake and for the gospel's, who shall not receive a hundred fold now in this time … and in the age to come, eternal life."—Mark 10:29–30

These Scriptures were very interesting to me at this point in life. My husband would become more and more depressed. Instead of me trying to meet his needs, I would just point him to God. I stopped allowing his depression to affect me. Every time he would talk to me about not being happy, I would tell him I could not help him. I learned that he could not meet my deep needs, and I could not meet his. However, he did not know how to turn to God, and he had no desire to. As a result, he lived away from the house. Every decision and conversation I had with him was for the sake of the gospel. I prayed daily for his salvation.

The Scripture said I would receive a hundredfold now in this time, and in the age to come, eternal life and I held on to that promise. The sword of Christ was separating the good and evil in my household. It would either bring my husband to repentance to Christ in this marriage, or it would not. But my priority had to be Christ.

Of course, the most precious reward for giving up my potential family for the sake of Christ is the eternity I would get to spend in His glorious presence. At that point, I felt like I had given up my husband and the children I would never have. However, there was the promise in this Scripture that if I put Christ first now, there would be some sort of reward now. It said I would receive a hundredfold now and eternal life in the time to come. It did not say "or." The essence of the verse is that I had to reorder my priorities so that Christ should be even more important than my family. I felt I had learned that lesson the hard way. I felt that I was persecuted daily by my husband for growing so close to Christ. He said he loved me, but he was not happy. Then he would move in and move out. It was always an emotional roller-coaster. The only reason I let it happen was for the sake of Christ and the gospel in the hopes that he would also find Christ. I could see his hopelessness and despair, but I could not help him. When I let my husband go at this deeper level, and when I put Christ first in my heart and mind, that was when I started to learn a little about contentment. Paul said in Philippians 4:11, "I have learned in whatever state I am to be content." I felt so close to this verse that I lived it each day.

Then it happened. I get the phone call. My husband said he loved me and wanted to move back in the house. It was amazingly ironic to me. I stopped trying to meet his needs, and he wanted to move back in. This had happened to me so many times, I realized that my husband did not really know what love was. I thought he must have run out of money or something, but he was moving back in. I was still convicted in my heart that I was the only true Christian he knew. My job was to be Christ in the world to Him. Jesus said we should forgive seventy times seven times, and God said He hated divorce. So we were living under the same roof again. He slept on the couch, and I slept in the bed. He lived his life, and I lived mine.

Except this time, we put some effort into going on dates. One Friday evening we went to a friend's house for dinner. Their teenage daughter and her girlfriend were there. They keep looking at me and snickering. I was aware that something was not right, as I know this is the one couple my husband had been spending time with while he was not living in the house. But there is nothing I can do about it. We had been married just about four years at this point. My life has been like this for three and a half years. I couldn't believe the Lord had this scenario going on for so long. The nice thing now is that I'm not emotionally tied to my husband. He is not the one meeting my deepest needs, God is.

I accepted the strife. I accepted the constant lack of direction. I turned it all over to God and let Him control the circumstances. In 1828, contentment was defined by Webster's Dictionary as a resting or satisfaction of mind. The word content meant rest or quietness of the mind in the present condition, satisfaction that holds the mind in peace, restraining complaint, opposition or further desire.

My desire to have children was still part of me, but I turned it over to God. My desire for a godly husband was still part of me, but I let God control that too. I tried to have the faith of a mustard seed and decided that even if I spent the rest of my life childless and married to my current husband, I would follow God and love God no matter what. Through much prayer, I turned my earthly desires over to God.

These four years were my first lesson in learning that God was in control, not me. It was a long lesson to learn. As soon as I truly accepted this lesson and circumstance, I discovered the verse Ephesians 3:20. It says, "Now to Him who is able to do immeasurably more than we ever imagined." God showed me how to have quietness in my heart by staying in my current situation. He gave me immeasurably more than I ever imagined He could. I had a very big God, and I was grateful to let the whirlwind of life keep going around me, and I just rested in God's presence. I would later find out that God had other plans that were even larger than I realized.

When we are on this Earth, we are always going to have a desire that cannot be fulfilled. Ecclesiastes 3:11 says, "He has made everything beautiful in its time. Also, He has put eternity in their hearts, except that no one can find out the work that God does from beginning to end." We were created for fellowship with God. We were created for eternity, and we will never fully have it on this Earth as we will never be fully united with Christ on this Earth.

We will never be fully content as we are waiting to be saved from this world. We are waiting for true fellowship with God. We are eagerly waiting with perseverance. Only God can fill that void, so we will never have 100 percent contentment in this world as we will never be 100 percent in the presence of God until we are in heaven or until Christ returns. The whole creation groans to be saved, and we are part of that creation.

"For we know that the whole creation groans and labors with birth pangs together until now. Not only that, but we also who have the first fruits of the Spirit, even we ourselves groan within ourselves, eagerly waiting for the adoption, the redemption of our body. For we were saved in this hope, but hope that is seen is not hope; for why does one still hope for what he sees? But if we hope for what we do not see, we eagerly wait for it with perseverance."—Romans 8:22–25 (New King James Version)

I learned to hope for what I could not see with my eyes. I hoped for my reward and eternity with Christ. I eagerly waited for it with perseverance. That meant that even though my circumstances were less than desirable, I decided to persevere. I could not control or change my circumstances, and my stubbornness in this regard was that the Lord had to be the one to take action. I learned that unless God was in control, life would only get worse. I would lose hope and I would not have a character that could wait in perseverance.

I held on to the promise that Jesus came so that we could have life and have it more abundantly (John 10:10). Jesus came to this Earth to give us an abundant life no matter what circumstance we are in. We can have the first fruits of the Spirit now. These are the only things that will give us any degree of true contentment as it can be experienced on earth.

Our lives in this world are but a vapor (James 4:13–17). God has knowledge and control of this world from beginning to end. Shouldn't we trust Him with the path we are to live?

While in prison Paul wrote, "I have learned in whatever state I am to be content" (Philippians 4:11). He had one hand chained to a wall and another hand chained to a guard. Previously, he wrote in the same letter, "I also count all things lost for the excellence of the knowledge of Christ Jesus my Lord, for whom I have suffered the loss of all things, and count them as rubbish, that I may gain Christ … and that I might know Him" (Philippians 3:8–10).

Even though he probably experienced contentment to a degree I can never imagine, he still said that to live and suffer for Christ's sake is good, but to die is also gain. Paul understood that there are better things to come, no matter what is experienced on this Earth. Paul understood that God had placed eternity in his heart. Paul understood that the gospel was expanding and peoples' lives were being impacted for eternity, because he was willing to suffer and live for Christ. He knew his life on this Earth was but "a vapor" and counted his present comfort as rubbish in comparison with someone coming to know the Lord. When we are Christians, and we die, we are united with Christ. Nothing can surpass that.

Divorce would not have given me contentment if it was outside the will of God. The Lord has an individually chosen path for each of us to walk. Taking action without God's lead would not have given me contentment. There always would have been something to cause my mind to not be at rest. I had to first learn that the only way to contentment was to follow God's leading. In essence, I had to sacrificially obey God, no matter what the cost.

"So it shall be when all of these things have come upon you, the blessing and the curse which I have set before you, and you call them to mind in all nations where the LORD your God has banished you, and you return to the LORD your God and obey Him with all your heart and soul according to all that I command you today, you and your sons, then the LORD your God will restore you from captivity, and have compassion on you."—Deuteronomy 30 (New American Standard)

Repeatedly in Scripture, the Lord promises to curse those who disobey Him and bless those who obey Him. It took me a very long time to learn this lesson. Deuteronomy 30 is just one example of the promises God made to Israel for obedience. Israel had disobeyed God and suffered the consequences. Another people group had enslaved them. However, God promised to restore them when they obeyed Him with all of their heart and soul. I was also enslaved to my sin. I was held captive by many of the beliefs in this world. It wasn't until I obeyed the Lord with all of my heart and soul that I started to taste freedom. The Lord left me in captivity long enough for the lesson to become a part of who I was. Loving God meant obeying God, no matter what the cost.

"Woe to him who quarrels with his Maker, does the clay say to the potter, 'What are you making?' Does your work say, 'He has no hands'?"—Isaiah 45:9

The Lord was making me into a woman with particular characteristics, and I had to learn to be molded without asking God what He was doing.

Chapter 7

Betrayal, Forgiveness, and Freedom

Previously, I talked about the desires of my heart, and how it led to a church trip to Egypt. I was separated from my husband during this time. Then, in the fall, he decided to move back to the house. Since I still did not know what to do when an unbeliever keeps coming back, I let him move back in again. However, the trip was already paid for and was coming in a couple months. When he moved back in, I made it clear I would be gone for two weeks. He did not express any concerns over that.

Two weeks before I was scheduled to leave, a major hurricane hit our area. Work closed early. As nightfall approached, I heard the wind blowing strongly and trees limbs breaking, and the power went out. The funny part about this is that I don't even live near an ocean, and this was the most powerful storm to ever hit our area. I went without power in my house for ten days. The street across from me had power restored within forty-eight hours. This was just another challenge before my trip. Four days before my flight, power was finally restored. I felt that there must be something special about this trip for such a strong spiritual battle to be taking place prior to my departure.

Finally I was in the plane on my way to Egypt. I was so excited to be sharing the love of Christ with the Muslim women in whatever way I can. I had read so many articles about how mistreated most Muslim women are. I felt I could relate to their unequal marriages in a way most American women could not. Even though I was Christian, my husband was not. He did not love me; he just used me for financial support and a roof over his head and a portion of his physical needs. He was not a person who was capable of love. The Muslim faith also seemed to produce men who were not really capable of loving their wives. I so looked forward to showing compassion toward the women I would come in contact with.

I found Egyptians to be amazingly warm and friendly individuals. Everywhere we went, there was warmth toward us. We had an armed guard with us at all times in case we were attacked. Each conversation was typical, and the Egyptians usually started it.

It would go something like this:

> "Are you an American?"
> "Yes, I am."
> "Are you a Christian?"
> "Yes, I am a Christian."
> "I am a Muslim."
> "Oh, what do you believe?"
> "I believe the Koran."
> "Oh, I believe that God loves you. Do you believe that?"
> "No, I don't believe that."

And, that would be the end of the conversation. At the time of my visit to Egypt, individuals were identified on their ID cards as Christian or Muslim. In America, we are identified by the color of our skin (i.e. – Caucasian, American Indian, etc.). It was very natural for the Egyptians to ask this as their second question while in America, the answer to your background is more obvious and rarely asked.

The Muslims we encountered believed in a god who was far away. Their faith did not have the Holy Spirit that came and lived inside of them to lead them, guide them and comfort them. Their faith did not have Jesus, who came to the world and experienced life the same way we do in order to die and show us the path to Heaven. Jesus took our punishment of death so we could go to Heaven and have life for eternity. They just had Allah who lived far away, gave instructions in the Koran and did not personally relate to them. If Allah was mad at you the day you died, and you still did everything the Koran told you to do, he might still send you to hell. He was not really a close and personal god with whom they could have a relationship. They did not know what it was like to have a loving relationship with God the perfect Father who loved you and sent His Son to die for you. My heart ached at the sadness of their faith. My faith gave me a personal relationship with a loving God who met my needs, and I so wanted to share with women how much strength this could give them in their situations. We were made for love, and many faiths do not produce love or a god who is close to them.

Chronicles describes a loving God: "If my people, who are called by my name, will humble themselves and pray and seek my face and turn from their wicked ways, then will I hear from heaven and will forgive their sin and will heal their land. Now my eyes will be open and my ears attentive to the prayers offered."—II Chronicles 7:14–15

During this time, the power of prayer became so real to me. It was the fifth day of our trip, and we toured a minaret that was thousands of years old. It was open for tourists to climb. There was a narrow, dark spiraling staircase to get to the top. Since it was about 105 degrees and I am claustrophobic, I sat down on the steps in the courtyard to enjoy the scenery while the rest of the group climbed to the top.

I watched the Egyptians walk by and relaxed my tired feet that were still swelling from the plane ride and high temperatures. I had on a long peach skirt, a three quarter-length tan shirt, and sandals to respect the conservative dress and culture I was visiting. I sat down on the historic blue tile steps that felt somewhat cool compared to the air temperature. I watched for my group to peek out at the top of the minaret so I could take their picture from the bottom.

I was awed by the Muslim religion. How awesome that they call their people to pray five times a day. You have to admire the discipline and commitment. They humble themselves by putting their forehead on the ground to pray. I truly admired and appreciated the reverence. I was also saddened that they felt they had to do something to earn salvation when salvation is really a free gift from God. Then, as I continued to meditate, I was saddened by how demonic the chanting sounded to me through the minarets during the call to prayer. If you ever watch a witchcraft movie where there is chanting, that is how the minaret calls to prayer sounded to me, especially since I did not know the language. As I sat there, I prayed that one day the minarets would be used to worship God with beautiful music.

About thirty seconds later, the ladies in our group started singing, "I Want to be a Living Sanctuary." Muslims on the street instantly stopped in their tracks and listened. The ones who spoke English looked at me and said, "Beautiful music." The ladies who sang were part of our church choir, so it was beautiful and echoing throughout the streets. I was so awed by the presence of God at this moment that all I could do was agree with them. To this day, this is the fastest answered prayer in my life.

A few days later, toward the end of the trip, two amazing things happened. When I was very young, I always wanted to see the Sphinx. Of course I never thought it would happen as I did not grow up in a family that traveled abroad or had lots of money to spare. I never thought I would set foot in a foreign country. Since studying astronomy in college, I also had the deep desire to see the Milky Way. From where I lived, it was not possible to see the Milky Way. In one day in Egypt, I got to see the Sphinx and the Milky Way. Talk about God fulfilling the desires of your heart. These were two desires I never related to God and truly never thought would be fulfilled.

Earlier that same day, I had climbed Mount Sinai. It took three hours to climb and one hour to descend. Some friends of ours who lived in Egypt told us that the Muslims believe that any prayer said at the top of Mount Sinai would be answered. Christians and Muslims both trace their start back to Exodus in the Bible. The Muslim peoples' faith comes from the bloodline of Ishmael, and the Christian faith comes from the bloodline of Isaac. They both share Abraham as their father, with different mothers.

While I don't tend to believe in myths, I thought this was interesting. It laid a burden on my heart to be sure to pray at the top of Mount Sinai. We rented camels and rode for an hour, though I'm not sure whether that made the trip easier or harder. The square saddle was not well cushioned, and I felt like I was sitting on two boards. Since I was brunette and the other ladies were blonde, they got padded saddles. The Muslim men were physically attracted to blonde ladies and had offered to buy them on several occasions. After a one-hour camel ride, the camels could go no further, and we started walking. I thought about Moses climbing the mountain to see God.

In my exhaustion after climbing in 100-degree heat straight up a mountain, I was not sure what to pray. However, the Lord quickly brought me to tears. I so deeply felt the presence of the Holy Spirit at the top of that mountain. One prayer was for my best friend, Katrina. She had been battling infertility for several years. Her first attempt at in vitro fertilization had failed, and she was considering another attempt. I prayed that the Lord would bless her and give her two babies at one time. I prayed for her to have a boy and a girl. Then I prayed for the most awesome, godly marriage in the world. At this point, I am praying this prayer while still married to an unbeliever.

Then came time to fly home. I returned home, and my husband met me at the airport. I was not really excited to see him but pretended to be. It would have been expected for him to pick up his wife at the airport after she had been gone for two weeks.

We made it through the holidays, and then New Year's came. He was distant and made it a point to not be home at midnight. I stayed on the couch until the ball dropped, phoned him several times, and finally realized he would not be coming home. I thought this very odd as one of his New Years' Eve traditions was to always be home by 11:30. At this point, I really started to push him to be a better husband. I made sure he knew that I thought it was wrong for him to disappear for New Year's and did not hide it from our friends either. Being a person who always avoided controversy in a marital situation, this was highly unusual behavior for me.

A few days later, on January 3, he dropped the bomb. Again we were sitting across from each other at the kitchen table. I had grown to despise these conversations. He told me that he had been through paternity tests, and that he had a three-month-old baby. He thought it was wrong for him to have a child by another woman when he would not have one with me, so he was leaving.

At first I thought it was the baby from his one-night stand. Then, a couple days later, I did the math. He had been cheating on me for a year and a half. I felt so betrayed and so free at the same time. I did have to make another concerted effort at forgiveness. I confronted him for putting my life in danger due to AIDS or who-knows-what else. But then I was free. I knew God would take care of me.

Finally, I could move forward with my life. This was the biblical reason I needed for a divorce. The Lord made it clear to me it was time for me to be single, and I was ready in every way. I had been determined not to divorce until God took action. I could move forward without guilt.

Now came the time to learn about forgiveness. Dictionary.com states that forgiveness is "to grant a pardon to a person and to cease to feel resentment against someone who has done you wrong." The world really focuses on the feelings of forgiveness. The Bible tells us the heart is deceitfully wicked. I think that if we really had our way about it, we would never forgive anyone for anything they have done to hurt us.

So now was a new year. I was driving home from work daily to an empty house. I had a feeling of freedom, yet the hurt was very deep. I was excited and apprehensive about the next direction of my life.

As soon as I pulled into the driveway, I saw the cut-down trees in the backyard that I have to find a way to chop into firewood. I walked in the front door to be greeted by the 110-gallon fish tank that I now have to take care of myself. I smell the odor of tobacco that I think will never go away since I wasn't the one who smoked. And there are the lingering belongings I am hoping will disappear soon so I can move forward with making the house my own.

I had many thoughts of forgiveness running through my mind. I had been forgiving him on an ongoing basis for hurting me over and over again over the past five years. It was the same way that I have to run to God and ask God to forgive me for sinning over and over again. Had I really forgiven my husband, or had I just gone through the motions? How do you forgive someone who has hurt you so deeply? Did I feel resentment toward him? Did it matter how I felt? Am I damaged goods for the rest of my life?

"And when you stand praying, if you hold anything against anyone, forgive him, so that your Father in heaven may forgive you your sins."—Mark 11:25 (New International Version)

"Do not judge, and you will not be judged. Do not condemn, and you will not be condemned. Forgive, and you will be forgiven."—Luke 6:37

"Therefore, I tell you, her many sins have been forgiven—for she loved much. But he who has been forgiven little loves little."—Luke 7:47

"Bear with each other and forgive whatever grievances you may have against one another. Forgive as the Lord forgave you."—Colossians 3:13

"For I will forgive their wickedness and will remember their sins no more."—Hebrews 8:12

The Bible tells us that God became man in the form of Jesus Christ. Jesus lived through pain and suffering. He can understand everything we go through. But, for weeks I wondered, *How could Christ know what it was like to have a husband cheat on you like that?* Christ was never married. Christ never became one flesh with a woman. How could He know what it was like to feel the way I was feeling? Then I was reading through my Bible one evening, and the answer hit me like a ton of bricks! Christ was betrayed with a kiss!

He knew what it was like to be betrayed in an intimate way. Christ was betrayed with a kiss, and I was betrayed with a kiss. So as my high priest, he could intervene for me. He could understand what I had been through. He could understand my emotions. In Matthew 26:24, Jesus says to Judas, "You would betray the Son of Man with a kiss?" Judas was one of the twelve disciples. To everyone around, Judas was one who was closest to Christ. Judas handled the money for the disciples. He was in the inner circle that Christ had chosen to keep closest to Him. Then Christ was betrayed by an intimate act of friendship. His close friend kissed Him in order to turn him over to those who would mock, beat, and kill Him. Judas only outwardly pretended to follow, love, and obey Christ. The same as my husband only outwardly pretended to be my husband. Inwardly, my husband was not committed to me. And, inwardly, Judas was never committed to Christ.

I was so relieved to be praying to someone who understood. Then I started to understand that He also knew what it was like to lose someone with whom He was one flesh. You see, Christ had always been joined to the Father. Then, when the sin of the world was poured out on him for three hours, the Father had to turn his face away. In Mark Chapter 16, Jesus cried out from the cross, "My Father, My Father, why have You forsaken Me?" Christ had spent eternity being one with the Father, and now He was not.

The whole point of marriage is for us to have an earthly example of what it is like to be one with another person. So, Christ experienced the ultimate pain of separation much more than I ever could.

Now I had to learn what true forgiveness was. It was time for the Lord to restore what the locusts had eaten. I found a lawyer and started the paperwork for a divorce based on the grounds of adultery. The nice thing was that the laws in my state did not require a waiting period since we did not have children together. I was free to move on, and the Lord is the one who did it, and I did not have to wait any longer. It was the ideal situation for a divorce. Since my husband already had the paternity tests, the evidence was complete.

Within three months, I was divorced. I got a settlement for a small portion of the money he owed me so I could pay off some credit card debt; the house was never in his name so he signed off all right to that; and the majority of his stuff was moved off my property. I felt true freedom in a way I never thought possible.

The most surprising part of the situation was that any loyalty I had ever felt toward him was gone. My promise to the Lord had been fulfilled, and I no longer felt any obligation to protect him or even pray for him as my husband since he was no longer in that position. I wish I could describe the peace and freedom I felt.

During the process, he asked me to change the grounds of divorce from adultery, since he could go to jail for committing adultery. At the time, about twenty-two states in America still had adultery in their criminal statutes. While changes were made due to the Texas court decision making sodomy legal, our State continues to have adultery as a criminal offense. I had no guilt when I said I could not do that. I had to get a divorce for biblical reasons, and the reason had to stay "adultery." It was so nice to have God give me the strength to do that.

There is a lot of confusion in this world on the act of forgiveness. The most common expression is that people will "forgive but not forget." In order to experience true freedom from bitterness or resentment, I had to forgive all of my husband's actions toward me. I had to let go of those actions or I could become a bitter person.

In Charles Swindoll's book *Growing Strong in the Seasons of Life*, he writes: "Bitterness seeps into the basement of our lives like run-off from a broken sewer pipe. Every form of ugliness begins to float to the surface of those murky waters: prejudice and profanity, suspicion and hate, cruelty and cynicism. There is no torment like the inner torment of bitterness, which is the by-product of an unforgiving spirit. It refuses to be soothed, it refuses to be healed, it refuses to forget. There is no prison more damaging than the bars of bitterness that will not let the battle end."

In Matthew 18:21–35, Jesus tells a long parable on forgiveness. He tells of a man who has a debt that cannot be paid. If the man worked every day for the rest of his life, he could not earn enough money to pay the debt. But the king releases the man from the debt anyway. The man also has a servant who owes a much smaller debt. When the servant asks for forgiveness, the man throws the servant in jail until the debt can be paid. The king heard of this and is furious because his forgiveness was not extended to another person.

When someone wrongs us, we have a choice to make whether to obey God and forgive others or disobey God by not forgiving them. We are commanded over and over again in Scripture to forgive others. We are even commanded to extend love or compassion to our enemies. What really happens when we forgive someone else is that we are sharing the grace of God that was first given to us. Forgiveness is a decision we can make to be like Christ in this world, and it is a way to choose not to sin. The ability to obey God in the area of forgiveness is a step to be free from sin that traps us and ties us to worldly attitudes.

Forgiveness was the last step in my journey to be truly free from my husband. I could choose to hate him, but what good would that do me? I would live my life in a prison of hatred. Why would I want to waste my time with such negative emotions filling my day? I could choose to be filled with anger, but again, being angry would have done no harm to my husband. I would only have harmed myself.

"For if you forgive men their trespasses, your heavenly Father will also forgive you. But, if you do not forgive men their trespasses, neither will your Father forgive your trespasses."—Matthew 6:14–15

I knew I needed God's forgiveness, because I am human, and I sin every day. On a daily basis, I chose to forgive my husband. I forgave him for not loving me, not respecting me, not hugging me, not working, not helping with the cleaning, and not being part of the marriage relationship. I did not want a warped and dead Spirit because I had bitterness in my life. I wanted to go through life with love, joy, and peace filling my heart. It was actually easier to forgive my husband than to forgive myself. Many times in life, forgiveness is a decision, not a feeling. However, if I did not forgive my husband on a daily basis in this almost five-year marriage, I would have been a bitter person, being tormented by the actions of someone else. I did not need that torment.

"Who is a God like you, who pardons sin and forgives the transgression of the remnant of his inheritance? You do not stay angry forever but delight to show mercy."—Micah 7:18

God gave me hope, insight, joy, and a relationship with Him far greater than I would have imagined. I learned how to have a relationship with the God of the universe. I would truly give my life for that!

Chapter 8

Obedience is Better than Sacrifice

During the entire time I was married to an unbeliever, the Lord was teaching me one lesson: to love God is to obey God. This is the most important lesson I learned during these five years. I first learned that I must obey God. Then I learned how to obey God. This chapter will contain interesting stories from the Bible and the outcomes of obedience. Interwoven in these Scriptures are personal stories in which the Lord showed me His faithfulness if I obeyed Him. Obedience to God became the central theme of my life, and I hope it will become the central theme of your life as you read these powerful examples of truth from the Bible and my life. God is alive, and He is truly the same yesterday, today, and forever.

There is a story in the Old Testament where King Saul did not obey God several thousand years ago.

"'Now go, attack the Amalekites and destroy everything they own as an offering to the Lord. Don't let anything live. Put to death men and women, children and small babies, cattle and sheep, camels and donkeys.' Then Saul defeated the Amalekites. He fought them all the way from Havilah to Shur, at the border of Egypt. He took King Agag of the Amalekites alive, but he killed all of Agag's army with the sword. Saul and the army let Agag live, along with the best sheep, fat cattle, and lambs. They let every good animal live, because they did not want to destroy them. But when they found an animal that was weak or useless, they killed it.

"Then the Lord spoke His word to Samuel: 'I am sorry I made Saul king, because he has stopped following me and has not obeyed my commands.' Samuel was upset, and he cried out to the Lord all night long. Samuel said to Saul, 'Stop! Let me tell you what the Lord said to me last night.' Saul answered, 'Tell me.' Samuel said, 'Once you didn't think much of yourself, but now you have become the leader of the tribes of Israel. The Lord appointed you to be king over Israel. And he sent you on a mission. He said, Go and destroy those evil people, the Amalekites. Make war on them until all of them are dead. Why didn't you obey the Lord? Why did you take the best things? Why did you do what the Lord said was wrong?' Saul said, 'But I did obey the Lord. I did what the Lord told me to do. I destroyed all the Amalekites, and I brought back Agag their king. The soldiers took the best sheep and cattle to sacrifice to the Lord your God at Gilgal.'

"But Samuel answered, 'What pleases the Lord more: burnt offerings and sacrifices or obedience to his voice? It is better to obey than to sacrifice. It is better to listen to God than to offer the fat of sheep. Disobedience is as bad as the sin of sorcery. Pride is as bad as the sin of worshiping idols. You have rejected the Lord's command. Now he rejects you as king.'

"Then Saul said to Samuel, 'I have sinned. I didn't obey the Lord's commands and your words. I was afraid of the people, and I did what they said. Now, I beg you, forgive my sin. Come back with me so I may worship the Lord.' But Samuel said to Saul, 'I won't go back with you. You rejected the Lord's command, and now he rejects you as king of Israel.' As Samuel turned to leave, Saul caught his robe, and it tore. Samuel said to him, 'The Lord has torn the kingdom of Israel from you today and has given it to one of your neighbors who is better than you. The Lord is the Eternal One of Israel. He does not lie or change his mind. He is not a human being, so he does not change his mind.'

"Saul answered, 'I have sinned. But please honor me in front of the older leaders of my people and in front of the Israelites. Come back with me so that I can worship the Lord your God.'

"So Samuel went back with Saul, and Saul worshiped the Lord. Then Samuel said, 'Bring me King Agag of the Amalekites.' Agag came to Samuel in chains, but Agag thought, 'Surely the threat of death has passed.' Samuel said to him, 'Your sword made other mothers lose their children. Now your mother will have no children.' And Samuel cut Agag to pieces before the Lord at Gilgal. Then Samuel left and went to Ramah, but Saul went up to his home in Gibeah. And Samuel never saw Saul again the rest of his life, but he was sad for Saul. And the Lord was very sorry he had made Saul king of Israel."— I Samuel 15:3–34 (New Century Version)

To summarize the story, the Lord gave specific instructions to Saul. He told Saul to kill all the people and animals. In verse 9, the Lord's instructions were only partially followed because they did not kill the king and they did not want to kill the good animals, so they didn't. In verse 20, we see Saul rationalizing that he did obey the Lord. He says when talking to Samuel that the animals were brought back to sacrifice to the Lord . The Lord's instructions were specific; the offering God wanted was to have the king and all of the animals killed. In Saul's mind, he either rationalized not obeying God or truly convinced himself that he had. Then we see Samuel tell Saul that "to obey is better than sacrifice," and Samuel kills the king Saul was supposed to kill himself.

Jeremiah 17:9 tells us the mind is deceitful above all things. Saul had convinced himself that he did obey God. When confronted by Samuel, Saul states, "but I have obeyed the Lord." In actuality, he only partially obeyed the Lord by killing the bad and keeping the good. In this Scripture, we see the prophet telling Saul that disobedience is as bad as the sin of sorcery and that pride is as bad as the sin of worshipping idols.

We see in the Scripture that Saul began to think highly of himself. There is a saying that absolute power corrupts absolutely. Saul was the absolute authority in his day, and he became quite corrupt. The more we are able to do for ourselves, and the more highly we think of ourselves, the less we think of God. God is the only true power. Prior to marrying a man who was an unbeliever, I spent ten years thinking very highly of myself. I applied the world's wisdom that it is okay to date an unbeliever. I applied the world's wisdom that it is okay to live together before getting married to be sure it would work. I thought very highly of myself and little of God at that point.

During the course of those five years' of marriage, my source of wisdom changed. I started applying Scripture wholeheartedly to every decision I made. The Scripture clearly told me that "God hates divorce," and I applied this to my life for years. Every time someone would tell me I should seek a divorce, I would tell them that God hates divorce and the only time it's allowed is a biblical divorce, when an unbeliever leaves or commits adultery. It wasn't that I didn't want change in my life, but I wanted to obey God more. I prayed that the Lord would strengthen me, enable me to love my husband the way He commanded, and if it was His will, rescue me from my mistakes. The Lord left me in the situation until I learned all I needed to learn to be sure I would always do what I could to obey His commands.

In the Old Testament, the act of sacrifice can be related to our act of going to church. Sacrifice was how the Israelites repented their sins and worshipped the Lord. Today, we go to church to worship the Lord. However, the Lord does not want us to come worship Him on Sundays and then be disobedient to Him the rest of the week. To do so does not bring honor and glory to His name. The world and your neighbors know who goes to church. If there is no difference in how you live your life and how your neighbor (who does not go to church) lives his life, that just proves that it does not matter if God is involved in our lives. It proves that God is distant, does not care, or does not have the power to change lives when nothing could be further from the truth. To obey is better than sacrifice. When we obey, sin is overcome and the power of God is seen through us.

"But I show kindness to thousands who love me and obey my commands."—Exodus 20:6

"But I will be very kind for a thousand lifetimes to those who love me and obey my commands."—Deuteronomy 5:10

"Blessed is the man who fears the Lord, who delights greatly in His commandments. His descendants will be mighty on earth; the generation of the upright will be blessed. Wealth and riches will be in his house, and his righteousness endures forever. Unto the upright there arises light in the darkness; he is gracious, and full of compassion, and righteous. A good man deals graciously and lends; he will guide his affairs with discretion. Surely he will never be shaken; the righteous will be in everlasting remembrance. He will not be afraid of evil tidings; his heart is steadfast, trusting in the Lord. His heart is established; he will not be afraid, until he sees his desire upon his enemies. He has dispersed abroad, he has given to the poor; his righteousness endures forever; his horn will be exalted with honor. The wicked will see *it* and be grieved; he will gnash his teeth and melt away; the desire of the wicked shall perish."—Psalm 112

I don't know about you, but I need the Lord's kindness. It is clear that in order to receive the Lord's kindness, we must obey Him. Psalm 112 is a beautiful song of praise to the Lord. In the New Testament, Jesus said, "I have come that they may have life and may have it more abundantly." In Psalm 112, we see David worshipping the Lord, providing a picture of what an abundant life on Earth looks like. The first picture of an abundant life is that the man who fears the Lord is blessed. Proverbs tells us that fear of the Lord is the beginning of wisdom, and in Psalms we see the first step to being a blessed man (or woman) is to fear the Lord.

There are many examples in Scripture of descendants not following the Lord, but as a rule, those who walk with the Lord will produce generations of families that also walk with the Lord. In my family, I have been blessed with parents who love the Lord, both sets of my grandparents loved the Lord, and all my great-grandparents that I have been told stories about also loved the Lord. I can clearly see the Lord's work continuing through the generations. Taken out of context, verse 3 could be interpreted that if you love God, you will be rich with lots of material possessions. However, there are many Christians who have limited material possessions. They have things such as peace, love, joy, and contentment. There are also many rich people in this world with lots of material possessions who are more miserable than we can imagine. They worry about money, are addicted to drugs, or work twenty-four hours a day just to have more. All Christians have mansions waiting for them in heaven. What could be more rewarding than spending eternity in heaven in the presence of the God of pure love? That is how our righteousness endures forever.

Christians always have the light of Christ to follow. We always have hope in the darkness. Darkness is never able to overcome light. By fearing the Lord, we are able to share the wealth the Lord has given us, because God is our provider.

The best verse in this Psalm is that our hearts are steadfast, trusting in the Lord. Our circumstances can change, the world around us can fall apart, but we always have the Lord to lean on regardless of our circumstances. And as the Psalm continues, we see the spiritual battles in the end.

The New Century Version of the Bible says it best. The wicked will see it and become angry. Many times I struggle with how successfully wicked people seem to be living. They don't appear to have the same struggles I have. They seem wealthier. But I know where they will be in the end.

Author Charles Spurgeon expands on the last verse better than I ever could: "The tenth and last verse set forth very forcibly the contrast between the righteous and the ungodly, thus making the blessedness of the godly appear all the more remarkable. The wicked shall see it and be grieved. The ungodly shall first see the example of the saints to their own condemnation, and shall at last behold the happiness of the godly and to the increase of their eternal misery. The child of wrath shall be obliged to witness the blessedness of the righteous, though the sight shall make him gnaw his own heart. He shall fret and fume, lament and wax angry, but he shall not be able to prevent it, for God's blessing is sure and effectual. The heat of his passion shall melt him like wax, and the sun of God's providence shall dissolve him like snow, and at the last the fire of divine vengeance shall consume him as the fat of rams. How horrible must that life be which like the snail melts as it proceeds, leaving a slimy trail behind. Those who are grieved at goodness deserve to be worn away by such an abominable sorrow. 'The desire of the wicked shall perish.' He shall not achieve his purpose, he shall die a disappointed man. By wickedness he hoped to accomplish his purposes—that very wickedness shall be his defeat. While the righteous shall endure forever, and their memory shall be always green; the ungodly man and his name shall rot off from the face of this earth. How wide is the gulf which separates the righteous from the wicked, and how different are the portions which the Lord deals out to them. O for grace to be blessed of the Lord! This will make us praise him with our whole heart."

As I continue to grow in my Christian walk, I have a keen understanding of the words "gulf that separates the righteous from the wicked." My outlook on life is different. My values are different. My decisions are different. A great example of this is how I spend my time compared to how most spend their time. I spend my time listening to Christian music that glorifies God, going to church, or using my leave from work to go on mission trips. I see others spending their time listening to rock or country music that glorifies sex and relationships, playing sports, and using their leave to go to the beach and do nothing. It is just a different perspective on what is important. Do we honor God, or do we honor self? I am the one who is looked at as having "bad" values because my values are not the same as the world's values.

2 Timothy 3:12 says, "Yes, and all who desire to live godly in Christ Jesus will suffer persecution." Timothy was a letter written by Paul toward the end of his life to his friend and student who would carry on the sharing of the gospel after Paul died. Paul was one of the early persecutors of the Christian church prior to his salvation. In the book of Acts, Paul was in their midst offering approving glances for the stoning of the first Christian martyr. He knew what it was like to persecute, and he knew what it was like to be persecuted. Yet once he discovered Jesus, there was no turning back.

We see the perfect example of the wicked becoming angry because of godly choices in the book of Daniel: King Nebuchadnezzar made a gold statue ninety feet high and nine feet wide and set it up on the plain of Dura in the area of Babylon. Then he called for the leaders: the governors, assistant governors, captains of the soldiers, people who advised the king, keepers of the treasury, judges, rulers, and all other officers in his kingdom. He wanted them to come to the special service for the statue he had set up. So they all came for the special service and stood in front of the statue that King Nebuchadnezzar had set up. Then the man who made announcements for the king said in a loud voice, 'People, nations, and those of every language, this is what you are commanded to do: When you hear the sound of the horns, flutes, lyres, zithers, harps, pipes, and all the other musical instruments, you must bow down and worship the gold statue that King Nebuchadnezzar has set up. Anyone who doesn't bow down and worship will immediately be thrown into a blazing furnace.'

"Now people, nations, and those who spoke every language were there. When they heard the sound of the horns, flutes, lyres, zithers, pipes, and all the other musical instruments, they bowed down and worshiped the gold statue King Nebuchadnezzar had set up. Then some Babylonians came up to the king and began speaking against the men of Judah. They said to King Nebuchadnezzar, 'O king, live forever! O king, you gave a command that everyone who heard the horns, lyres, zithers, harps, pipes, and all the other musical instruments would have to bow down and worship the gold statue. Anyone who wouldn't do this was to be thrown into a blazing furnace. O king, there are some men of Judah whom you made officers in the area of Babylon that did not pay attention to your order. Their names are Shadrach, Meshach, and Abednego. They do not serve your gods and do not worship the gold statue you have set up.'

"Nebuchadnezzar became very angry and called for Shadrach, Meshach, and Abednego. When they were brought to the king, Nebuchadnezzar said, 'Shadrach, Meshach, and Abednego, is it true that you do not serve my gods nor worship the gold statue I have set up? In a moment you will again hear the sound of the horns, flutes, lyres, zithers, harps, pipes, and all the other musical instruments. If you bow down and worship the statue I made, that will be good. But if you do not worship it, you will immediately be thrown into the blazing furnace. What god will be able to save you from my power then?'

"Shadrach, Meshach, and Abednego answered the king, saying, 'Nebuchadnezzar, we do not need to defend ourselves to you. If you throw us into the blazing furnace, the God we serve is able to save us from the furnace. He will save us from your power, O king. But even if God does not save us, we want you, O king, to know this: We will not serve your gods or worship the gold statue you have set up.'

"Then Nebuchadnezzar was furious with Shadrach, Meshach, and Abednego, and he changed his mind. He ordered the furnace to be heated seven times hotter than usual. Then he commanded some of the strongest soldiers in his army to tie up Shadrach, Meshach, and Abednego and throw them into the blazing furnace.

"So Shadrach, Meshach, and Abednego were tied up and thrown into the blazing furnace while still wearing their robes, trousers, turbans, and other clothes. The king's command was very strict, and the furnace was made so hot that the flames killed the strong soldiers who threw Shadrach, Meshach, and Abednego into the furnace. Firmly tied, Shadrach, Meshach, and Abednego fell into the blazing furnace. Then King Nebuchadnezzar was so surprised that he jumped to his feet. He asked the men who advised him, 'Didn't we tie up only three men and throw them into the fire?' They answered, 'Yes, O king.' The king said, 'Look! I see four men walking around in the fire. They are not tied up, and they are not burned. The fourth man looks like a son of the gods.' Then Nebuchadnezzar went to the opening of the blazing furnace and shouted, 'Shadrach, Meshach, and Abednego, come out! Servants of the Most High God, come here!' So Shadrach, Meshach, and Abednego came out of the fire. When they came out, the governors, assistant governors, captains of the soldiers, and royal advisers crowded around them and saw that the fire had not harmed their bodies. Their hair was not burned, their robes were not burned, and they didn't even smell like smoke! Then Nebuchadnezzar said, 'Praise the God of Shadrach, Meshach, and Abednego. Their God has sent his angel and saved his servants from the fire! These three men trusted their God and refused to obey my command. They were willing to die rather than serve or worship any god other than their own. So I now give this command: Anyone from any nation or language who says anything against the God of Shadrach, Meshach, and Abednego will be torn apart and have his house turned into a pile of stones. No other god can save his people like this.' Then the king promoted Shadrach, Meshach, and Abednego in the area of Babylon."—Daniel 3

It was the practice in those days to conquer other lands and take the best of the conquered to serve as slaves in new countries. It was easier to keep people under control if they were not in their home countries. Shadrach, Meshach, and Abednego were slaves taken from the land of Judah. They were moved to Babylon, and they had earned favor with the king. As a result they were appointed to a high position. Then, the king thought very highly of himself, and made an idol that everyone had to worship. By bowing to this idol that the king created, the people were also pledging their loyalty to the king. Even though the king had done good things for Shadrach, Meschach, and Abednego, their loyalty was to God. They did not bow to an idol knowing it would be offensive to God.

We see a classic reaction from the king. He was angry and confronted them. The king felt they owed him their allegiance since he had placed them in positions of leadership. Their response was a true statement of faith. Verse 17 says, "The God we serve is able to save us from the furnace. He will save us from your power, O king. But even if God does not save us, we want you, O king, to know this: we will not serve your gods or worship the gold statue you have set up." Are you so sure of your faith that you would tell someone holding a gun to your head, God will save me from that bullet, but even if He does not save me, I will still not worship another"? Do you have this type of unwavering faith and confidence in God? As the story continues, we see that God chose to save them from the furnace, and Nebuchadnezzer recognizes God as more powerful than any other god. According to Pastor Randy Hahn, this applies to our lives, that when we obey God, other people have the opportunity to see God's power working in our lives.

Shadrach, Meschach, and Abednego had spent many years of their lives as teenagers in Babylon being taught the wisdom of the world. They were taught the traditions and customs of the Babylonians who worshipped many other gods. Yet they did not lose their faith and wisdom from the one true God.

In her book *Daniel: Lives of Integrity Words of Prophecy,* Beth Moore describes the story by saying, "We can be delivered from the fire, and as a result, our faith is built. We can be delivered through the fire, and as a result, our faith is refined. Or, we can be delivered by fire into His arms, and as a result, our faith is perfected."

The world has much "wisdom" today that is in complete contradiction to God's word. We are saturated by this wisdom, and somehow, like Shadrach, Meschach, and Abednego, we must find a way to always seek the truth from God's word. This wisdom teaches there are many paths to heaven, or other paths to heaven, or all religions are equal, or that we must look to our inner selves for peace. I learned the hard way that in order to have an abundant life that begins on Earth, I must find God's instructions in the Bible. The Bible is the best instruction manual ever written on how we should live our lives.

I have had many individuals tell me that not every situation is in the Bible. Examples include which job I should take, where I should live, where my kids should go to school, and who I should marry. My experience is that for every decision I have ever had to make, I prayed, searched the Scriptures, and allowed the Holy Spirit to lead me. Using this method, the Lord has always given me the desires of my heart and the means to accomplish those desires.

Here is what Jesus taught us about obeying the Lord:

"I have obeyed my Father's commands, and I remain in his love. In the same way, if you obey my commands, you will remain in my love. I have told you these things so that you can have the same joy I have and so that your joy will be the fullest possible joy."—John 15:10

"We can be sure that we know God if we obey his commands. Anyone who says, 'I know God' but does not obey God's commands is a liar, and the truth is not in that person. But if someone obeys God's teaching, then in that person God's love has truly reached its goal. This is how we can be sure we are living in God: whoever says that he lives in God must live as Jesus lived."—1 John 2:3

"This is what God commands: that we believe in his Son, Jesus Christ, and that we love each other, just as he commanded. The people who obey God's commands live in God, and God lives in them. We know that God lives in us because of the Spirit God gave us."—1 John 3:23

"Loving God means obeying His commands. And God's commands are not too hard for us, because everyone who is a child of God conquers the world. And this is the victory that conquers the world-our faith. So the one who wins against the world is the person who believes that Jesus is the Son of God."—1 John 5:3

First we see that Jesus came to this Earth and set the example for us. He obeyed God. By obeying God, He remained in the Father's love. Then He goes on to say that if we obey Him, we remain in His love. I have found that life has much more joy if I obey God, even if it is not the easiest road to walk according to the world's standards. When I disobeyed God, I ended up in a horrible marriage. When I obeyed God in my horrible marriage, I was released from it. As a teenager, my house had much strife, because I did not obey God by honoring my parents. There would have been much more peace and a better outcome had I learned early to obey God.

There is nothing more awesome than having the Spirit of God living inside you. I encourage you that if you do not have the desire to obey God's commands, spend some time in prayer and determine why this is the case. Does the Spirit of God live in you? I have lived my adult life obeying God's commands, and I have lived life disobeying God's commands, and there is no other option for me than to wholeheartedly obey God's commands without doubt and without hesitation.

"And have you forgotten the encouraging words God spoke to you as His children? He said, 'My child, don't make light of the LORD's discipline, and don't give up when He corrects you. For the LORD disciplines those He loves, and he punishes each one He accepts as his child.' As you endure this Divine discipline, remember that God is treating you as His own children. Who ever heard of a child who is never disciplined by its Father? If God doesn't discipline you as he does all of His children, it means that you are illegitimate and are not really his children at all. Since we respected our earthly fathers who disciplined us, shouldn't we submit even more to the discipline of the Father of our spirits, and live forever? For our earthly fathers disciplined us for a few years, doing the best they knew how. But God's discipline is always good for us, so that we might share in his holiness. No discipline is enjoyable while it is happening—it's painful! But afterward there will be a peaceful harvest of right living for those who are trained in this way.'"—Hebrews12:5–11 (New Living Translation)

I recently attended an *In His Garden* Bible study that expanded on this scripture vividly with an example from nature. Chickadees are birds that grow up quickly. The first few days, mama chickadee spends most of her time sitting on the nest providing warmth and safety for her babies to grow, as God provides a home for each of us to grow in. After about a week, the babies have all their feathers. When it is time to leave the nest, the parents stop feeding the baby chickadees. The babies cry for food, yell and complain, but the parents know what is best.

We are the same when God withdraws His blessing from us due to sin. After getting all of their feathers, it is time for baby chickadees to learn to fly. The parents know the babies will never leave the nest as long as they keep bringing food to them. We also are unwilling to step out of our comfort zone when God makes everything too easy for us.

The big day comes for the babies to leave. Momma and Daddy keep flying back and forth from the nest to a nearby cedar tree. There were five babies in this nest that needed to leave. Momma flies into the nest, raises quite a racket, and two babies follow Momma out. They were obedient the first time. When we are lazily living in sin, some of us obediently obey God with the first rebuke and start bearing fruit again. I was much more stubborn than that in my walk with the Lord.

The chickadee parents continued flying back and forth to get the other three to leave the nest. After about half an hour, chickadee number three left. Some of us ignore God's gentle rebuke but slowly let go of our sin when God speaks sternly and chastens us. I also did not respond to God's original gentle rebuking or chastening.

Two hours go by, and the other two babies are still stubbornly sitting on the chickadee nest. The babies that did not follow their parents were punished that day with hunger. The three that left the nest got to imitate their parents feeding and got to eat. The babies finally left the nest after the second day. The parents loved their babies enough to rebuke them and finally made their babies miserable enough to get them to do what was best for them.

Another example is a grapevine, with branches hanging down in the dirt. The vinedresser has not come by to pick up the branches and prune them or tie them up properly. The branches hanging in the dirt no longer receive air and light and will soon die if not taken care of. The dirt is like sin for us. If we choose to live in the dirt of sin, we will soon not be able to hear the Holy Spirit or bask in the light of God's sun. If we continue to choose to stubbornly live in sin, the relationship we have with God will begin to die. In Hebrews 12, we see that God always disciplines us in a way that will produce good.

God speaks in various ways to "prune" us. He speaks through our conscience (our internal principles), preaching from the pulpit, and conviction of right and wrong by the Holy Spirit. He starts out by rebuking us gently with a sense of dissatisfaction with ourselves, agitation, or a sense of that things are not quite right. If we continue in our sin, God will chasten us using things such as anxiety, frustration, increasing pressures at work and home, or with health or money issues. If we continue to live in our sin, we force God to scourge us, to inflict punishment on us, just like the two chickadees that were hungry for two days.

In my life, I forced God to inflict punishment on me. He kept His word to me. My work situation was terrible as I put earning money over spending time with God, my marriage was terrible as I chose to marry someone who did not love God, and my finances were terrible as I did not tithe. It wasn't until I started learning to obey God as an adult that I started learning what joy and blessings were. It is clear to me that God gently rebuked me, then He chastened me, and then He scourged me. Yet I still continued to sin. However, I am so thankful to be His child. If He did not love me, I would not have had any of these problems in my life and I would still be following the world's wisdom.

Pat and Jane's story

I met Pat and Jane in the later part of their life. Their three children were grown, and they attended church together. Pat and Jane went to a small church, and Pat was the happy man who always gave SweeTarts candy to all the kids at the end of the church service. Pat went on at least two mission trips per year, and every time he talked about missions, tears of joy would come to his eyes. Pat loved God.

This was not always Pat and Jane's story. Much earlier in their life, Pat was in the military and was not a believer, and Jane took the kids to church by herself. Pat and Jane believed in "until death do us part." There was no other way out of marriage. Jane met with a group of women and prayed earnestly for her husband's salvation. The Lord worked a miracle and changed Pat from being an unbelieving husband to the man with a heart for missions.

The greatest part of this story is that the Lord gave Jane's daughter the same gift of a husband who loves the Lord, though it did not start out that way. Jane's daughter married a man who was an unbeliever, and they had three children together. He would attend church with her, but he was quiet and not involved in the worship. Jane's daughter had a beautiful spirit for missions as well. Yet something was holding her back. From an onlookers' perspective, it wasn't obvious what that was until one day, her husband came before the church for salvation and baptism. Now the whole family leads an "angel" food ministry at this very church, hoping others will find Christ as well.

Chapter 9

Post Divorce, Dating, and Restoration

So began my life as a single, divorced woman. I was free to date but didn't really have the desire to date. The desire of my heart was to just be with the man the Lord wants me to marry, and no one else. I felt too old to play the field or the dating games. I had to learn what God's intentions were for dating.

There are many Christian philosophies on the appropriate way to date.

One is "friendship dating." This allows men and women to spend time together as friends. They meet somewhere for dinner or spend the day together as friends in a neutral location. Many times, there is a close friendship that builds in the relationship. But there is never the opportunity to cross the boundary of being anything more than friends unless someone is led in that direction. In this philosophy of dating, it is okay to spend time with one person of the opposite sex in a one-on-one relationship, as you are just friends.

I have observed several problems with this particular philosophy. One problem is that even though the friendship boundary is well established, someone usually gets hurt. It is almost impossible for men and women to spend time together in a one-on-one situation without someone getting emotionally attached. What happens if one of the individuals actually found his or her mate? That leaves the other person out in the cold without his or her friend to spend time with anymore. It is certainly not appropriate for them to go out as friends anymore when one is now invested in a relationship. To me, this equation just leads to disaster.

The other thing to think about is that if you are spending time with your friend of the opposite sex, but your potential spouse is aware that you are in these situations, he may never ask you out on a date as he sees you are already invested in a relationship. He may not know you are just friends. He may not want to get in the middle of your friendship. Your reputation may be tarnished even though all boundaries are firmly established and you are just friends with this person.

Another philosophy on Christian dating is "group dating." Men and women get together in groups of four, six, or eight and go out on group dates. Individuals are paired up for the evening to get to know each other. The next time, the pairing may be different. Again, the purpose is to establish friendships and get to know individuals of the opposite sex. All boundaries are firmly established and this gives men and women the opportunity to interact in a safe group setting. This option also takes the formality out of dating. Generally, each person pays his or her own way. Again, friendships may be invested with individuals of the opposite sex, and once someone finds his or her mate, the group dynamic may change. This style of dating also has some of the same risks as friendship dating, without the one-on-one interaction.

Another philosophy on Christian dating is to live life with a mindset as if you are already married. You respect all other individuals of the opposite sex with appropriate boundaries as if they were married. This was my mindset on dating. It keeps you loyal to your spouse even if you don't know who he is yet . You can pray for your spouse. You can pray for his character, his relationship with God, and for wisdom in identifying who he is. This mindset establishes boundaries with individuals of the opposite sex. If you are in a Christian singles group or church setting, you can establish friendships with individuals of the opposite sex in those settings, yet not outside those settings. It gives you the skill of interacting with those of the opposite sex in a respectful way in circumstances that are flexible enough to allow the relationship to continue or not continue after you find your mate, if you both continue in the same social circles. The friendship can continue or fade without someone getting hurt.

This philosophy also keeps you from emotionally investing yourself in relationship after relationship until you find the right person. Even if you are friendship or group dating, you are giving away a piece of yourself by sharing who you are with someone who does not have a vested interest in your future.

"The body is not meant for sexual immorality but for the Lord, and the Lord for the body. By his power, God raised the Lord from the dead, and he will raise us also. Do you not know that your bodies are members of Christ himself? Shall I then take the members of Christ and unite them with a prostitute? Never! Do you not know that he who unites himself with a prostitute is one with her in body? For it is said, 'The two will become one flesh.' But he who unites himself with the Lord is one with him in spirit. Flee from sexual immorality. All other sins a man commits are outside his body, but he who sins sexually sins against his own body. Do you not know that your body is a temple of the Holy Spirit, who is in you, whom you have received from God? You are not your own; you were bought at a price. Therefore honor God with your body."—I Corinthians 13b–20 (New International Version)

This is an amazing and convicting passage of Scripture about dating and boundaries. The first aspect, of course, is physical boundaries: "Flee from sexual immorality." It does not say put up an appropriate boundary, it says run the other direction. The most amazing part is that when you really look at the meaning of the passage, it says that when you unite with a prostitute, you are married at the point you unite. Then that prostitute is united to the body of Christ. We, as Christians, are all one body in Christ. It is an overwhelmingly amazing concept to think that as soon as I am physically united to someone, the Lord views us as married. Then, since the two become one flesh, the body of Christ is either lifted up or defiled.

What a powerful conviction against premarital sex. After you have sex with one person, you and the whole body of Christ are married to that person. If you have sex with anyone else, you are committing adultery, as you have already been united to the first person. How I wish these truths would be understood and taught to singles in the world today.

During my first round of dating as a teenager, I did not have this knowledge. After my divorce, it was easy to move forward with a mindset that I was married and would live life in a way that honors my husband-to-be, who I knew God had out there for me. If I could be faithful to someone who did not love me, it was not as challenging to be faithful to a future husband God would choose for me, even though I had not met him yet. I wasn't perfect at it and almost fell into the traps of friendship dating or group dating, but the Holy Spirit quickly convicted me of God's plan. I had to have faith in God to bring my husband to me in His timing. I received many crazy looks when I was single and tried to explain this philosophy, but in my observation of the single world, it worked better than any other philosophy out there.

You may wonder, *If I don't date, how am I ever going to meet someone?* It is up to God to bring someone into your life. "Seek ye first the kingdom of God, and all these things will be added unto you" (Matthew 6:33). As a single person, I had opportunities I never had as a married person. I was able to go on mission trips, prayer-walk in my community, help with mission conferences, and have two-hour quiet times with God. It was such a joyous time of refreshing my spirit.

"I would like you to be free from concern. An unmarried man is concerned about the Lord's affairs—how he can please the Lord. But a married man is concerned about the affairs of this world—how he can please his wife—and his interests are divided. An unmarried woman or virgin is concerned about the Lord's affairs: her aim is to be devoted to the Lord in both body and spirit. But a married woman is concerned about the affairs of this world—how she can please her husband. I am saying this for your own good, not to restrict you, but that you may live in a right way in undivided devotion to the Lord."—I Corinthians 7:32–35

This Scripture is saying that individuals who are not married are able to focus on the work of God. While I felt I was called to be someone's wife, I start to embrace this Scripture while still a single person. My quiet time is alive and active and everyone who knows me says I am running at full pace toward God. I pray for the salvation of various neighborhoods while walking through them, teach women's classes, and go on mission trips. I did not have to worry about the way I spent my time affecting anyone else. I am able to focus on the Lord as never before.

On July 4 of that year, I attended a Christian singles get-together. One of the men owned a small house by the river and hosted a party every year for the group. We spent the evening taking turns on jet skis, swimming, cooking out, and socializing. As the evening closed, the singles group leader approached me and asked me to co-teach a small group in the fall. I had been drawn to other small groups but was avoiding them as I wasn't sure of the structure. I told her I would pray about it. I hesitated because I didn't know who the co-leader would be, and I wanted to be sure of the Lord's leading. At the beginning of August, I would let her know I was willing to teach.

Susan explained the structure to me. She said that all small groups have a male and female co-leader. She said, "I think I'm going to set you up to teach with Steve Taylor. Have you met him before?" My answer was no. She went on to rave about what a great guy he is and that she has taught with him before. He is the vice mayor of Hopewell and a great drummer. She thought all of that would impress me, but I was not the type of person to be impressed by status. I felt hesitant about having someone I did not know come into my home in a spiritual leadership position. But I had agreed, and I decided to pray and give him a thorough once-over before we officially started teaching together.

During this same time frame in the Christian singles group, approximately fifty different men asked me out on a date. I was the new girl. While it was flattering, and I'm sure they all had the best of intentions, I found it emotionally exhausting. Generally, I would go to an event and meet several people. After the event, between one and four men would contact me and ask me out. They would get my contact information from an e-mail list. I had to pray every time someone asked me out. I would get an emotional high from being asked, and then frustrated because it never felt right. I needed so much wisdom from God to answer a simple question as to whether or not to go out with someone. It was challenging for me to be in this unexpected situation. These were all Christian men who I don't think would ever cross boundaries, and they were only interested in being friends at that point. But that was just not who I was. One thing that was a huge blessing to me was that if I could be loyal to an unfaithful husband, I could much more easily be loyal to a faithful one.

I had committed myself to not date unless I was sure it was going to be the person I was going to marry. I really was not interested in giving my emotions to anyone I wasn't going to marry. I had spent four and a half years giving myself to someone who would not be my husband for life. I did not want to give any more of myself away. I did not want to waste the emotions on building friendships with men who were not going to be my life partner. I knew I couldn't build friendships with them and keep close friendships with them after I was married. Even though the world would not agree, that would be disrespectful to my husband.

Finally, in early August, I cried out to the Lord during my quiet time. I listened to music and engrossed myself in worship. I read my devotional and Bible, and I wrote in my journal. The Lord took over my pen. This particular day, I prayed a frustrated prayer to the Lord that I needed God's divine intervention regarding my dating life. I really did not know what to do, and I did not want to keep being so frustrated.

The Lord gave me a clear answer. I started writing, "When the man God has chosen to be my husband asks me out on a date, he will say, 'I have been praying, and I feel the Lord has led me to ask you out on a date.'" I felt at ease with this answer to my prayer.

Later in August, I went to a Willow Creek Ministries conference that was paid for by the singles group. They planned to develop leaders for the group. I met my small group co-leader at the conference, and we exchanged information so we could get together to pick a topic and work out details for teaching the group.

On Labor Day, I went on a trip to the beach with the singles group. Again, another person asked me on a date. He was a nice person, but he did not say the right words. I explained to him that I did not want to be in a one-on-one situation with someone of the opposite sex unless I was serious about dating this person as a future marriage partner. He responded positively to my honesty and said he appreciated my character. I felt really good about the Lord's leading.

I had another experience with a much more negative response. I had not been perfect with my friendship boundaries throughout the summer, as I had met someone for dinner only as a friend on a couple of occasions. This completely violated my rules, but I rationalized it because he usually met other women for dinner on a routine basis. When I explained my feelings to him and my commitment I had made to myself, he was very hurt. This really supported my original assumption that men and women can't be just friends without someone getting hurt.

After this prayer, and firming up my boundaries, I felt confident in moving forward in life. I met my co-leader for dinner, and we picked a topic to teach. I used all my professional skills as an auditor and fraud investigator to ensure I was co-leading with someone who had character I could trust. Some of his answers were very political in nature. At first glance, he was a true politician. He gave me both sides of an answer, and it took several questions to find out where he stood on some issues. By the end of dinner, I felt great about co-leading the small group with him. Later, I had a phone conversation with my friend Katrina and told her I could marry him. She thought I was saying I could marry someone like him. But for some reason, I felt I could marry this man. Then that was the end of that thought process for a while.

We became good friends throughout the teaching process. I got a glimpse into his spirit and love for the Lord over the weeks that he taught, and he got a glimpse of my spirit and love for the Lord on the weeks I taught. Toward early November, I started to feel a strong draw to him and would like for him to ask me on a date. However, other than a great friendship on Monday nights and occasional planning for the group, we did not have much contact otherwise. I started praying about him asking me on a date. Yet it didn't seem to be coming to fruition.

As a result, I make the decision to go to the foreign mission field on a permanent basis. I had been drawn to the mission field, but I did not feel I was meant to serve alone. I kept waiting, but the draw to the mission field kept getting stronger. I felt really out of place in my current situation. I finally prayed to God. I decide it did not matter if I was in Egypt, India, on some small island somewhere, or in America. If God wanted me to be married, He will bring me to my husband. I picked a date to go to the mission board to fill out an application. I started making phone calls to get my house ready to sell. I knew it would take a year of evaluation before I actually made it to the field.

Then, in December, Steve and I got together to talk about our next small group. We had agreed to teach together again next spring. He gave me a Christmas present but did not ask me out. I was encouraged but disappointed at the same time. It seemed strange that he would give me a Christmas present. I had no other opportunities to communicate with Steve except to meet him for dinner. So I made an exception in this situation. It would be clear to any onlooker that we only met once every four months to go over teaching material.

During this time, I talked to my friend Wendy from church. She has the most beautiful, sweet spirit of anyone I have ever met. I talked to her about the mission field, about my friendship with Steve, and about how I wasn't sure what God was doing. At one point, she made the comment, "When a Christian man falls in love, you'd better watch out!" I will never forget the sweetness, excitement, and passion with which she makes this comment. And oh how right she was.

This comment caused me to meditate on the difference between Christian and non-Christian men. Non-Christian men date many women. They generally do not establish boundaries of no friendships with other women while they are married or dating. This causes their emotions and affections that should be saved for their wife to be spread among many women. Even if they are loyal to their wives, they tend to commit adultery with their eyes or emotions, even if they do not physically commit adultery. They also don't have the selfless love of an all-powerful God flowing through them. They have not experienced God's forgiveness, thus they are not able to forgive. In contrast, Christian men, convicted to find just the right spouse, generally do not date very many women until God leads them. They have all this bottled-up passion and excitement that God has given them that they are saving for one very special woman. They are aware of their need for a helper the way God designed, and they wait for their helper until God brings her into their life. All of this friendship, love, and emotion is just waiting to be poured out on a very special person.

Steve and I once again meet for dinner to discuss our next small group. He ate blueberry pancakes. The next day, he e-mailed me and said, "I don't know what I enjoyed more, the blueberry pancakes or your company." I then knew I could encourage him a little—or a lot. I felt an unexplainable draw toward him. If I didn't encourage him, he probably would not ask me out. *But what if he doesn't say the right words?* I thought. I decided to give him a little encouragement and responded in e-mail, "Your company was the highlight of my evening." We met for lunch a few days later to finalize the teaching discussion, and toward the end of the conversation, he said, "I've been praying, and I feel the Lord has led me to ask you on a date." It felt like I had just been proposed to. The Lord was bringing to fruition my prayer on the top of Mt. Sinai. However, I did not share that secret with him right away.

Our first date was on Christmas Eve. We got together to play some board games, as all restaurants close early on this day. He spent Christmas day with his family and I spent Christmas day with mine. Steve was also involved in a leadership role in a youth ministry at his church. I expected to be kept at a distance until he knew where the Lord was leading, but he invited me to a New Years' Eve get together for his youth group. They have a bonfire at one of the other leaders' houses. It was a different situation for me to suddenly be in a Christian leadership position by assisting him in his role providing leadership with the youth group. In addition, I knew I was setting an example for dating that would be observed by all those in attendance. It was convicting to suddenly feel like the world's eyes were on you. The evening went well, and our relationship progressed.

One month later, my good friend Wendy was moving to Atlanta to get married. I was invited to the wedding, and I really wanted to attend and be part of this huge event in her life. I invited Steve to go with me, which was presumptuous two weeks into our relationship. However, I knew that we would be married at some point, and I wanted the women in my life who had been my mentors and sustainers for so long to meet this man that God had brought into my life.

Steve was hesitant when I invited him on the trip. He compared love to when it starts snowing: it doesn't cover the ground right away. You get a flurry, and after some time the ground starts to get covered. Then, much later, once there is an accumulation of snow, that is when you know you are in love. He finally decided to go on the trip to Atlanta with me. It was an eight-hour car ride with just the two of us to get to know each other. We talked nonstop all the way down.

Wendy had arranged separate sleeping arrangements for Steve and me. I was privileged to stay in a house with a married couple who had known Wendy since she was a child. Their house was full of God's peace, and I will never forget them. At Wendy's wedding, there was a huge snowstorm and ice storm that kept many of the guests away, so it ended up being a smaller wedding than she had planned. For Steve and me, the storm was just another blessing from the Lord as we reflected on Steve's analogy about snow falling. It snowed more frequently that winter than I can ever remember for our part of the country.

In March, Steve proposed to me. He had planned to take me horseback riding for my birthday and present me with a wedding ring. He had been told that one of the first questions everyone asks is, "How did he propose?" So he wanted it to be special. However, once he finally got the wedding ring, he was so excited that he could not wait to ask me. He took me to a special place that his dad use to take him to when he was still alive. It was snowing. He talked about how the snow was covering the ground and read I Samuel 18:1 to me: "Now when he had finished speaking to Saul, the soul of Jonathan was knit to the soul of David, and Jonathan loved him as his own soul." Then he explained how his soul had been knit to my soul and that he would like me to be his wife. It was the easiest yes to marriage as I knew this was the man God had chosen to be my husband.

Later, Steve and I read the Bible together, and we ran across God arranging a marriage the same way almost in the very beginning of time. We saw that God was interested in every aspect of our lives, including whom we marry.

Genesis 24 explains how a bride for Isaac was found: "Now Abraham was old, well advanced in age; and the Lord had blessed Abraham in all things. So Abraham said to the oldest servant of his house, who ruled over all that he had, 'Please, put your hand under my thigh, and I will make you swear by the Lord, the God of heaven and the God of the earth, that you will not take a wife for my son from the daughters of the Canaanites, among whom I dwell; but you shall go to my country and to my family, and take a wife for my son Isaac.'

"Then the servant took ten of his master's camels and departed, for all his master's goods were in his hand. And he arose and went to

Mesopotamia, to the city of Nahor. And he made his camels kneel down outside the city by a well of water at evening time, the time when women go out to draw water. Then he said, 'O Lord God of my master Abraham, please give me success this day, and show kindness to my master, Abraham. Behold, here I stand by the well of water, and the daughters of the men of the city are coming out to draw water. Now let it be that the young woman to whom I say, Please let down your pitcher that I may drink, and she says, drink, and I will also give your camels a drink—let her be the one You have appointed for Your servant Isaac. And by this I will know that you have shown kindness to my master.'

"And it happened, before he had finished speaking, that behold, Rebekah, who was born to Bethuel, son of Milcah, the wife of Nahor, Abraham's brother, came out with her pitcher on her shoulder. Now the young woman was very beautiful to behold, a virgin; no man had known her. And she went down to the well, filled her pitcher, and came up. And the servant ran to meet her and said, 'Please let me drink a little water from your pitcher.'

"So she said, 'Drink, my lord.' Then she quickly let her pitcher down to her hand, and gave him a drink. And when she had finished giving him a drink, she said, 'I will draw water for your camels also, until they have finished drinking.' Then she quickly emptied her pitcher into the trough, ran back to the well to draw water, and drew for all his camels. And the man, wondering at her, remained silent so as to know whether the Lord had made his journey prosperous or not."

Verses 21–49 tell how Abraham's servant approaches Rebekah's family and asks for her to marry Isaac. Verse 50 is the response: "Then Laban and Bethuel answered and said, 'The thing comes from the Lord; we cannot speak to you either bad or good. Here is Rebekah before you; take her and go, and let her be your master's son's wife, as the Lord has spoken.'"

Steve and I were married on July 1 of the same year. The following year, Steve became mayor of the city of Hopewell, and as his wife, many individuals called me the First Lady of Hopewell. The lessons learned many years ago that my husband would be known in the gates from Proverbs 31 resonated with me to the depth of my being. I never thought the Lord would put me in such a public position.

A year later, our daughter was born, and fifteen months after that, our son was born. The Lord fulfilled the desires of my heart that I had previously turned over to Him about having two children by the age of thirty-five. I was thirty-five when my second child was born.

"Now to Him who is able to do immeasurably more than we have ever hoped or imagined."—Ephesians 3:20

The most amazing thing God did for me was answer my prayer at the top of Mt. Sinai. I had prayed for two things. I prayed for my best friend to have twins, a girl and a boy. I prayed for the most awesome, godly marriage in the world. Three weeks before my wedding day, I helped host a baby shower for my best friend. Her babies were to be named Josiah and Susanna and are now a little more than a year older than my children. To this day, I consider my marriage and Josiah and Susanna to be direct answers to my prayer at the top of Mt. Sinai. What other explanation could there be for this timing? God is so alive, so powerful, and so amazing, and every day I become more amazed by His power. The more I learn about Him and the closer I become to Him, the more I realize I can spend my whole lifetime growing closer to the Lord and never stop being amazed by Him.

Afterword

"For all Scripture is given by inspiration of God, and is profitable for doctrine, for reproof, for correction, for instruction in righteousness, that the man of God may be complete, thoroughly equipped for every good work."—2 Timothy 2:16-17

The Bible is the most amazing book I have ever read. It is our instruction manual for life on this Earth. It is the living word of God, sharper than any two-edged sword. It teaches truths about God and about this world, and the principles upon which we should build our lives (doctrine). It shows us that we are sinners who need Jesus in our lives each and every day (reproof). It shows us how to change our lives to bring glory and honor to God (correction). It gives us a road map to righteousness and enables and prepares us to be a mirror of Christ for someone in this world who may otherwise never see Him.

For the almost five years I was in my first marriage to an unbeliever, the Lord humbled me. The Lord gave us Christ as a human example of how we are to live our lives. And we are commanded to be holy as Christ was holy. As I reflect on Christ's life on Earth, I am continually humbled that I will never be able to be as holy as Christ. I am also, many times, scared about what that could mean. Christ spent eternity in heaven. Then, at a particular time, He was placed in the virgin's womb. He grew inside a woman as a fetus and then experienced being born. Then He allowed someone to care for Him, feed Him, and teach Him to walk and talk. He became a carpenter with all the cuts, blisters, and bruised thumbs that come from that vocation. He lived a poor life, with much fewer modern conveniences than we have today. He walked everywhere. His earthly brothers, sisters, and the people from His hometown denied him. He was betrayed by one of His closest friends. All of his closest friends (disciples) abandoned Him the night He was arrested. Then He experienced a humiliating death on the cross. He separated Himself from eternal unity with God just for me. Jesus voluntarily humbled Himself. After three days, he conquered death to be exalted to the right hand of God. He conquered sin, death, and all of its consequences, but not because it saved Him, but because it saved me. This is the example God tells us to follow.

In many ways, all Christians can tell some similar story about how God humbled them before their ministry moved forward. The Lord spent years humbling me in order to prepare me to become exalted. You can humble yourself voluntarily, or the Lord will humble you involuntarily if you are His child. God allowed me to stray and follow my own path. He allowed me to live the consequences of my decisions, and then He eventually rescued and exalted me into a new life. He gave me compassion for women married to non-believers even though I naively said as a child, "I will never marry anyone who doesn't go to church with me." God gave me a bad marriage in the world's eyes so I could love and not be loved in return. He made me utterly dependent on Him. He showed me how to die to myself and to my desires in order to give me new desires in my heart. He showed me the ways of the world and where they led, and then He showed me His ways and where they led. Only then could He exalt me and give me a life better than I ever could have imagined. He gave me a wonderful second husband who loves me passionately and is a respected leader in the community. He fulfilled my dream of having two children by the age of thirty-five. He gave me a personal relationship with Him. He allowed me to go on mission trips and tell others about Him so they too can experience God in all His splendor.

Conclusion

As I reflect on the path God led me on over the past ten years, I can testify that every word of God's Scripture is true. Every promise He made that directly related to my path in life has come true. Many passages reflect God's judgment when you disobey Him.

One area of obedience is to treat your body as a holy temple of God. God promises that if you sin against your body in which the Holy Spirit dwells, He will destroy you.

"Do you not know that you are a temple of God and that the Spirit of God dwells in you? If any man destroys the temple of God, God will destroy him, for the temple of God is holy, and that is what you are."—1 Corinthians 3:16–17 (New American Standard Bible)

While I was a believer, and God would hold true to His promise of saving me in the end, I made many mistakes in how I treated my body. Through living with my first husband prior to marriage, I did not obey the Scriptures to save myself for marriage. As a result, God humbled me into wanting to obey Him. He left me in the fire for many years until I would obey Him no matter how hard it was. I learned that the Spirit of God did dwell in me, and that I should have obeyed God in regard to sexual relationships. God destroyed me in every way in this area. My husband committed adultery on me for years, and I spent years loving someone while not being loved in return. Adultery is a sin that destroys the person committing the sin, destroys his or her spouse, and destroys the family. God created the family as a beautiful picture of our relationship with Him. It seems to me that Satan is the happiest when he can destroy a Christian's life through this sin.

"But Jesus went to the Mount of Olives. Early in the morning, He came again into the temple, and all the people were coming to Him; and He sat down and began to teach them. The scribes and the Pharisees brought a woman caught in adultery, and having set her in the center of the court, they said to Him, 'Teacher, this woman has been caught in adultery, in the very act. Now in the Law Moses commanded us to stone such women; what then do You say?' They were saying this, testing Him, so that they might have grounds for accusing Him. But Jesus stooped down and with His finger wrote on the ground. But when they persisted in asking Him, He straightened up, and said to them, 'He who is without sin among you, let him be the first to throw a stone at her.' Again He stooped down and wrote on the ground. When they heard it, they began to go out one by one, beginning with the older ones, and He was left alone, and the woman, where she was, in the center of the court. Straightening up, Jesus said to her, 'Woman, where are they? Did no one condemn you?' She said, 'No one, Lord.' And Jesus said, 'I do not condemn you, either. Go. From now on, sin no more.'"—John 8:1–11 (New American Standard Bible)

In the New Testament, the temple of God is the church. Christians are the living stones of the church. Even as much as God promises judgment on those who destroy the temple of God, there is just as much balance in the Bible in that when we repent, God delivers grace. That does not mean there will not be earthly consequences to our mistakes, but what we do see is that even when we sin, God gives us grace. The church leaders of Jesus' day did not know what grace was. In the story of the adulterous women, they tried to get Jesus to stone a woman who was caught committing the act of adultery. Instead, Jesus showed them their sin and commanded the woman to go and sin no more. When I was living with my first husband-to-be, I tried to put myself in a situation to go and sin no more by getting married. The route I took was not the route God wanted me to take. I should have humbled myself, moved back home, and required him to marry me before continuing to act as his wife. However, I did not humble myself in this regard, so the Lord humbled me.

"Now therefore, here is the king whom you have chosen and whom you have desired. And take note, the Lord has set a king over you. If you fear the Lord and serve Him and obey His voice, and do not rebel against the commandment of the Lord, then both you and the king who reigns over you will continue following the Lord your God. However, if you do not obey the voice of the Lord, but rebel against the commandment of the Lord, then the hand of the Lord will be against you, as it was against your fathers."—I Samuel 12:13 (New King James Version)

As we can see from this passage, the nation of Israel was also considered to be children of God who made bad choices. At this point in the Scripture, Israel rejected God as their King and asked for an earthly king to be appointed over them. The Lord responded by giving Israel what they asked for. The nation had to live with their choice for thousands of years by having earthly kings rule over them. Every choice we make has an earthly consequence. The earthly consequence can bring God's blessing or it can bring God's judgment that we will have to live out on this Earth.

In my case, I made bad choices. Then I learned how to make good choices in the sight of the Lord. The first good choice I made was to obey God's word and stay married until God changed the course of my life. A better choice would have been to not marry an unbeliever to begin with, but I could not turn back the hands of time. I had to live with the consequences of my choice. However, once I started making wise choices based on faith in God, life started to turn a better course for me.

God's grace was sufficient for me to live through the consequences of the decisions I made. I had to stop sinning, and once I learned to obey God, His hand of protection was on me for many years. I did not get any life-threatening illnesses through the adultery my husband committed for years, and I gained a new spiritual makeover where individuals hardly recognized me. Then, in God's timing, the Lord provided a way out. God could have chosen to be glorified through leaving me in my first marriage for the rest of my life, but He chose a different path. Words cannot begin to express my appreciation to God for changing my life.

Living Together

At this point, you may be wondering what I think about those currently living together. The first step to obedience to God is the hardest to take. However, as I reflect on all the opportunities the Lord gave me over the years, I had ten years' prior to marriage to take the first step of faith. I never took that first step and had to live with the consequences of my decision for many years. Living together is a sin, and I should have stopped sinning as soon as the Lord started speaking to me. The Lord told the adulterous woman to go and sin no more. Regardless of the circumstances, the first step is to stop sinning or to stop living in a situation the Lord considers sinful. There is a way out, but it requires faith and obedience and reliance on God to make a lifestyle change. If you are living together or contemplating living together, my advice to you is to go and sin no more. Find a way to obey God right away and treat your body as a holy temple of God. As we learned earlier, the consequences of living with someone not only affect your body as the temple of God but every other person in the temple of God as well. We are all united in Christ. From an early view, it may seem there is no way you have the individual strength to stop the relationship that is dishonoring God. It doesn't require earthly strength. It just requires faith. God will give you the strength to bring honor to His name.

Questionable Activity in a Marriage

There are two biblical reasons for divorce. One is adultery (Matthew 5:32) and the other is when an unbeliever leaves the marriage (I Corinthians 7:15). Five years into my current marriage, the Lord chose to reveal to me wisdom I did not have in my first marriage. You will recall that I did not know what to do when an unbeliever returned to a marriage. Even though I wanted to seek help for destructive behaviors, I did not know where to turn or what to do. I did not have the wisdom or emotional strength that I have now. I Peter 2:13-14 says, "Therefore, submit yourselves to every ordinance of man for the Lord's sake, whether to the king as supreme, or to governors, as to those who are sent by him for the punishment of evildoers and for the praise of those who do good."

I wish I had known how to apply this Scripture to marriage many years ago. Without getting into the intricacies that we should disobey the law when it causes us to sin (i.e., don't worship other gods if the government requires you to do that like the choice Daniel had to make, or laws that don't allow you to attend church or pray at sporting events or allow homosexual marriage), when laws are put in place, we should obey them. As a Christian, I had an unbelieving husband who left the marriage. When he returned, I should have set boundaries that required some basic scriptural principles be met. Some of these additional boundaries could have included the principals in 1 Peter 2:13–14 ("Submit yourselves to every ordinance of man for the Lord's sake: whether it be to the king, as supreme; or unto governors, as unto them that are sent by him for the punishment of evildoers, and for the praise of them that do well"), having a job, and regular church attendance prior to moving back in. I did not have to allow him to move back into the house if he was not willing to implement these principals as an ongoing part of his life. I was blessed enough that my husband did not bring his new acquaintances directly to our home. Other women may not have that blessing. My knowledge was limited at the time I was in the situation.

The Lord chooses to work in different ways in everyone's lives. At the time I was going through my struggles, I did not understand that I was actually enabling my husband to continue in a lazy, self-destructive lifestyle. The one boundary I set for him was to not cheat on me. I allowed all of his other irrational and self-destructive behaviors to continue. Since the Bible did not support his lifestyle, I did not have to support it either since he had already left me as an unbeliever.

If your husband is causing or forcing you to sin against God in any way, whether it is through sexual sin, being exposed to drugs, or some other situation, Scripture is clear that you are first responsible to obey God by not participating in those things. If I had obtained this knowledge during my prior marriage, I do not think I would have pursued divorce since I did not know about the adultery until the end. I would have used this knowledge to require a lifestyle change prior to his moving back into the house and continuing as husband and wife.

Christian Woman Married to Non-Christians

There are many levels of marriage relationships in this world today. Regardless of how awesome the marriage is, I can't imagine that any Christian woman does not have the desire to be in a marriage where her husband is also a Christian. This is a deep-rooted desire whether the woman reveals it to others or not. Some of these marriages are wonderful by the world's standards and some are abusive.

For the marriages that are wonderful, I just want to encourage each woman to take the Scriptures in this book and apply them to your lives. Allow the love of God to flow through you. Follow the perfect marriage manual that God has written just for you. Create a sanctuary for your husband. As a human, your husband will never be able to completely meet your needs, regardless of his faith. Release him from meeting the needs that only God can meet, and just simply love and respect him with a chaste and gentle spirit. Allow God to save him, and just be his wife.

One of my biggest challenges while being married to an unbeliever was to envy all the women who came to church with their husbands. I knew in my heart of hearts that I was coveting what someone else had, but it was still a challenge. I did not want someone else's husband, but I wanted their situation. What I have learned over many years is that every challenge we have in life is an opportunity to trust God with the big picture. He can see the past, present, and future all at the same time, and all we can see is each second at a time. He must know something that we don't know, and we have to trust Him.

Rebecca's Story

Rebecca is a good friend who I have known for about ten years. We went to church together for many years in the same women's Bible fellowship class. Then I switched to a different church for a few years, and now the Lord has brought us together again at a new church. Rebecca epitomizes my thoughts of a gentle and quiet spirit. Rebecca always appears sweet and content, especially with her husband. During prayer request time, she would pray for her husband's pain relief in relation to a particular disability.

I knew Rebecca for at least three years before finding out that her husband was not a believer. I always thought he did not come to church because he wasn't physically able to. Over the past ten years, Rebecca's daughter, son-in-law, and grandchild have started loving God and faithfully coming to church. It was a huge miracle in her life. I don't think anyone but God knows the prayers she prays on a daily or even hourly basis for her husband to find salvation. Rebecca has not changed over the past ten years, and she has not given up. The desires of her heart are for her husband to find salvation.

Only once in ten years has the Lord given me a glimpse of Rebecca's spirit, in which she too would love to have her husband as the spiritual leader in the family. I greatly admire Rebecca for her respect of her unbelieving husband.

For the marriages that are to unbelievers and are also awful or abusive, I wish I could follow the world's advice and say, "Get out and get to some place safe as fast as you can." Please know that I spent years wanting to follow that advice. However, I was not and have not been able to find that wisdom in Scripture anywhere.

The wisdom I could find in Scripture was Psalms 37:4–5: "Delight yourself also in the Lord, And He shall give you the desires of your heart. Commit your way to the Lord, Trust also in Him, And He shall bring it to pass."

The Lord has a unique path for every woman to live. There are biblical principals to apply in every marriage, and only the Lord knows how He is going to free you from your present situation. Your freedom can come in an abundant lifetime on this earth, or it will come in an abundant lifetime in heaven. The world will tell you that you are abused and don't have the ability to make a good decision. Scripture says just the opposite.

"For God has not given us a spirit of fear, but of power and of love and of a sound mind."—2 Timothy 1:7

If you are abiding in God and God says you are to stay married, then the safest thing to do is to stay married. If God clearly says it is time to leave due to illegal activity, non-biblical activity (abuse, adultery, homosexuality), then the safest thing to do is leave and trust God for protection. Safe does not always mean easy or trouble-free. Safe does not always mean physically or emotionally safe. Safe is designed from an eternal perspective. Am I living under the grace of God? There are so many examples of people following the will of God only to end up in horrible circumstances. The apostle Paul was nearly beaten to death over and over. All twelve disciples, except for John, died the death of martyrs.

Missionaries all over the world have given their lives for the sake of the gospel. In the movie *End of the Spear*, based on a true story, five male missionaries give their lives trying to reach a violent tribe in Ecuador. All the missionaries had families, including Nate Saint's wife, Marjorie, and their son, Steve. Marjorie did not plan on having her husband killed while on the mission field, their young son in tow. Also in that group were Elisabeth and Jim Elliot. Jim's desire of his heart was to locate an un-reached group of people, and he did. On the day of his death, his baby girl was ten months old. Elisabeth was following the desires of her heart in missions, but she also did not expect to lose her husband.

In the book of Esther, she was living in a foreign land, gathered as a virgin to be introduced to the king of Persia as a potential wife, and married the king. As wonderful as this sounds, she was then called by God to risk her life to save the lives of the Jews by approaching the king without being summoned. Even though she was his wife, the king could have had her killed for approaching him without permission.

I am saying all of this to say you must first obey God. In order to obey God, you must know what it is God wants you to do in relation to your situation. The only way to do this is to diligently search the Bible and read devotionals to know the desires of your heart God has given you. God gives us the desires of our hearts, and it will be clear to you. My encouragement to you is that God has promised to give you wisdom if you ask for it.

My heart's deep desire during my first marriage was to obey God no matter what the cost. I knew God hated divorce. I truly desired a biblical divorce, but only if it was through no action of my own. The only way to do this was to have the unbeliever leave or commit adultery. After almost five years of waiting, God freed me from my marriage through my unbelieving husband leaving me because he had a three-month old baby with someone else. It does not get any more biblical than that! Scripture does not promise to release us from earthly consequences of our decisions or to change our earthly circumstances. It does promise us that the Holy Spirit will be with us in the midst of our circumstances. If we assume we are going to model the life of Christ in this world, we can expect no more than to give our lives for someone else to be introduced to the gospel. Christ died a brutal death in order for us to go to heaven. Only God can communicate with you the path you are to walk to bring Him honor and glory. In the process, He can be glorified through all you say and do.

Christian Woman Married to Christians

Christian women married to Christian men can be living the same wonderful marriages and the same awful marriages as Christian women married to non-Christian men. Every marriage has similar and unique challenges and opportunities for growth. This section is specifically written for Christian women whose husbands are putting God first in their marriages, doing their best to be Spiritual leaders in their household, and serving in some sort of ministry.

After my divorce, I received the question many times whether I thought I would ever marry again since my first marriage had been so horrible. Many times, people expressed how they thought I must have a low expectation of marriage. However, I continued praying for my husband daily utilizing the book *The Power of a Praying Wife.* I also had a list of approximately forty interests and character traits that were important to me. As evidenced by my prayer on the top of Mt. Sinai, I would answer the "marriage" question by saying I had very high expectations of any future marriage.

I must say that Christian marriage is as wonderful as I imagined. It is also infinitely more difficult than I imagined. If you are married to one of the godliest men you know, you are married to someone who is committed to Christian ministry. This means many hours away from home for the sake of eternity. While he truly loves you, he is still incapable of meeting your deepest needs. It takes a very strong, godly woman to support a Christian man in ministry. Many times we must share our husbands with other individuals while we want them all to ourselves.

And, if you have children, this means that much of the wife's ministry time is focused on being a helper to her husband by being devoted to managing many things around the house and taking care of the children. I have been doing this while working full-time as well. We women truly live under the curse. We are tempted in every way to think that we should have equal external ministries, and the world teaches us that if we stay home with the kids to help our husbands, something is wrong. I have learned just the opposite after five years of my second marriage.

I have observed in my marriage that if I put being a helper to my husband as a top priority, we both have a ministry. If I don't humble myself and submit to the Lord by first being a helper to my husband, then both of our ministries are much more limited. My husband's ministries continue, but my ministry becomes almost stagnant, as I'm not living the priorities the Lord has given me.

Our marriages and our ministries are only as strong as the weakest individual in the marriage. God created a beautiful thing when He created marriage in the Garden of Eden. After creating this beautiful union, God gave us the Bible to teach us how marriage works best, and it is the best relationship manual ever created. I encourage all women to allow God to mold you, prune you and bring you through the fire by the reading and application of His living word – the Bible. For your worth will be far above rubies, your husband will praise you, and your children will rise and call you blessed.

About the Author

Kim came to know the Lord as a young child. She attended Christian school until the eighth grade and then attended public school. Kim's life story is a modern-day example of being hard hearted toward the instructions from the Word of God, wishing that all those mistakes had not been made, and then having a miraculous and unexpected change in circumstances.

Her first marriage to an unbeliever was a shining example of being "unequally yoked." Four years into the marriage, Kim discovered her husband had been committing adultery. They were then divorced. The Lord then exalted Kim into being married to one of the godliest men she has ever met, and she was finally able to savor the love of a Christian man.

Kim and her husband, Steve, wrote their own wedding vows based on the scriptural mandates in marriage and to love the Lord your God with all your heart, soul, and mind. They have a son and daughter who are fifteen months apart in age. They are now raising their children to love the Lord with all their hearts, souls, and minds.

In addition to following God's command to show Jesus to the world, Kim has written *Humbled and Exalted,* fulfilling God's command for older women to teach younger women the Word of the Lord.

Bibliography

Augsburger, Myron S. *The Preacher's Commentary: Matthew.* Nashville, Tennessee: Thomas Nelson, page 59. February 12, 2004.

Chambers, Oswald. *My Utmost for His Highest.* Michigan: Oswald Chambers Publications, 1992.

Colson, Charles and Nancy Pearcey. *How Now Shall We Live?* Illinois: Tyndale House Publishers, Inc. 1999.

DeMoss, Nancy Leigh. *Lies Women Believe: And the Truth that Sets Them Free.* Chicago: Moody Press, 1991.

Dillow, Linda. *Calm My Anxious Heart.* Colorado: Navpress, 2007.

Hahn, Randy. *Great Stories of the Bible Sermon: The Fiery Furnace.* Colonial Heights, Virginia. September 19, 2010.

Keller, Timothy. *Counterfeit Gods.* New York: Dutton, 2009.

Harley, Jr., Willard F. *His Needs Her Needs.* Michigan: Fleming H. Revell, 1994.

http://www.jesusplusnothing.com/

http://www.proverbs31woman.com/

Lucado, Max. *In the Eye of the Storm A Day in the Life of Jesus.* Tennessee: W Publishing Group, 1991.

Moore, Beth. *Breaking Free Making Liberty in Christ a Reality in Life.* Tennessee: Broadman & Holman Publishers, 2000.

Moore, Beth. *Daniel Lives of Integrity Words of Prophecy.* Tennessee: Lifeway, 2006.

Omartian, Stormie. *The Power of a Praying Wife.* Oregon: Harvest House Publishers, 1997.

Prentiss, Elizabeth. *Stepping Heavenward.* Massachusetts: General Books, LLC, 2009.

Spurgeon, Charles H. *The Treasury of David, 3 volume set: Classic Reflections on the Wisdom of the Psalm.* Peabody, MA: Hendrickson Publishers, page 297.

Swearingen, Charlotte, et al. *In His Garden.* Colonial Heights Baptist Church, Colonial Heights, Virginia: 2008, p. 45.

Swindoll, Charles. *Growing Strong in the Seasons of Life.* Grand Rapids, Michigan: Zondervan Publishing, 1994.

Weaver, Joanna. *Having a Mary Spirit.* Colorado, Waterbrook Press, 2006.

Webster, Noah. *Dictionary of the English Language.* Chesapeake: Foundation for American Christian Education, 1828.

Scripture Index

CPSIA information can be obtained at www.ICGtesting.com
Printed in the USA
BVOW05s0032040315

390141BV00001B/96/P

9 781615 078677